BAG BAZAAR

25 Stylish Bags to Sew in an Afternoon

MEGAN AVERY

Illustrations by Shino Urano

POTTER
CRAFT
New York

646.48
A

To all the crafty ladies who come into my life.

You continue to inspire and motivate me.

Copyright © 2008 by Megan Avery

Published in the United States by Potter Craft, an imprint of the Crown Publishing Group,

a division of Random House, Inc., New York.

www.pottercraft.com

POTTER CRAFT and colophon is a registered trademark of Random House, Inc.

Library of congress Cataloging-in-Publication Data is available upon request.

ISBN: 978-0-307-40649-1

Printed in China

Design by Chi Ling Moy

Illustrations by Shino Urano

10 9 8 7 6 5 4 3 2 1

First Edition

ACKNOWLEDGMENTS

Special thanks to the following people: Mom, your constant can-do attitude teaches me to be an independent, strong woman and shows me I can do anything I put my mind to. Dad, your "Dad Ads" continue to show me so much love and support in all my endeavors. Grandma, your enormous fabric stash always kept me excited about my next project. Nina and Pop, your creative businesses showed me at an early age, you really can make a living doing what you love. To my sister Meredith, we've spent countless hours window shopping, all the while agreeing, "We could make that!" Ain't that the truth? To my sister Amanda, thanks for being one my biggest fans and best customers from the beginning. Emily, Heather, Ellen, Jess, Teresa, Perry, Karen, and Michelle, you are some of the best friends a girl could have. I don't know where I would be without you guys. Kumiko, thanks for creating most of the bag samples for the book and for being one of the most dependable people I know. Thanks to Danielle and Devon for treating my business as if it were their own.

CONTENTS

INTRODUCTION

Who doesn't love bags? They're completely functional parts of our wardrobe. Carrying everything we need for an evening out on the town to our most treasured possessions and our everyday essentials, bags do double duty—they serve a utilitarian purpose and they add style and splashes of color to any look. They carry our clothes and cosmetics when we travel, and our work and school necessities to and from our daily destinations. Today, the variety of bags out there spans a huge range, from those for stylishly carrying wine to a favorite BYO restaurant to those protecting laptops and electronic items from being scratched and damaged while in transit. They're also a quick and easy way to add some flair to an ordinary outfit.

However, as any handbag lover knows, they don't come cheap! I started making bags six years ago because I didn't have the money or the desire to drop hundreds of dollars—or more—on all the different styles of fun bags I came across. So often, I would see bags I loved and find myself saying, "I could make that so easily!" And I didn't have nearly the sewing and crafting experience I have now. I never went to fashion or design school; I never even took a sewing lesson to learn how to make bags. I did what you're doing right now. I picked up books and taught myself how to make designer-like bags for a fraction of what it costs to buy them. And the best part is that I could make them exactly the way I wanted to.

After designing, creating, and selling my line of handmade bags and totes for three years, I was overwhelmed by the interest so many people had in learning how to make bags for themselves. That's when I opened M. Avery Designs studio and started teaching Make-Your-Own-Handbag workshops. In these classes and at private parties, women who had little or no sewing experience learned how to make their own bags. I have seen the popularity of my

MYO workshop grow tremendously in the last three years. Since my staff and I opened the studio, I have taught over two thousand women of all ages in the New York metropolitan area to design and create their own handmade bags. This book reflects all the knowledge and experience I've gained through teaching others to make fabulous bags. I have taken the complications and intimidation out of the process by keeping the overall designs simple, and by adding depth and style using specialty fabrics, hardware, and details.

I put this book together so you can do just what I did. It's full of simple, fun-to-make patterns for handbags, purses, and specialty bags that you can whip up on a home sewing machine with very little sewing know-how. The patterns and projects included here are made from simple shapes and sizes that allow you to customize them with great fabrics, trims, and other notions. These simple bag shapes can go from funky to sophisticated, depending on your fabric and accessory choices. There's definitely something here to satisfy everyone's taste. I've also given you the tools to create your very own bag patterns (page 125). Use my pattern formulas to make a custom bag to your desired size and shape, depending on what you want to carry in it.

If you can use a ruler and you have some basic machine-sewing skills, which I review in the Basic Sewing Skills section (page 11), not only can you make bags, but you can design them yourself.

You'll also learn an array of useful techniques, including how to apply fusible and nonfusible interfacing; how to create and attach strong, sturdy straps; how to insert zippers and other types of closures; how to add pockets—both zippered and open; and many other clever strategies used in fashioning fabulous bags.

Making bags is incredibly easy and fun, and this book will serve as your guide and inspiration for creating cute, yet very functional accessories to carry just about anything. Get creative and have fun!

basic sewing and bag-making techniques

Before you begin, it's important to get your hands on a good sewing machine. If you don't already have one, check out garage sales, flea markets, and antiques stores. Even if the machine you find is not in perfect working condition, take it to your local sewing machine repair shop for a tune-up. Most likely, you'll still pay less for a sewing machine at one of these secondhand venues (plus the cost of the repair) than you would for a new machine at any department store. If you already own a machine, my recommendation would be for you to take it in for a tune-up before you get started. A sewing machine repair specialist will make sure everything is in working order, and save you loads of frustration down the line. If you have the luxury of being able to buy a brand-new machine, do your research. Head to a reputable sewing machine store and try out as many machines as you can. If you can't work on it first, don't buy it. Next, head over to your favorite fabric and notions store, pick up some fabric, or—better yet—grab a couple of cute tops that you aren't wearing anymore and recycle them into amazing new totes or clutches! You only need small amounts of fabric to create gorgeous bags that will be the envy of all your friends.

BOX STITCH FOR SECURING STRAPS

The box stitch is an excellent way to secure something like straps to your bag, which need to withstand a lot of wear and tear. The box stitch is a stronger stitch than most; that's why it's often used for attaching straps.

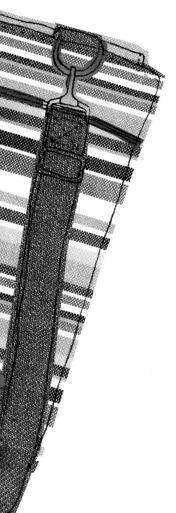

1. With tailor's chalk and a ruler, draw all 4 sides of a box, to the length and width desired with all sides roughly ⅛" (3mm) from the edge of the strap where you would like to box stitch.

2. Set the stitch length on your sewing machine so you're sewing short, tight straight stitches.

3. Stitch all the way around the drawn box.

4. Stitch from one corner of the box, diagonally across to the opposite corner.

5. Stitch across one edge of the box to get to the next corner.

6. Stitch from that corner of the box diagonally across to the opposite corner.

7. Stitch across the edge of the box again, until you have reached the corner where you started.

TOPSTITCHING

Topstitching is essential for bag-making. It's often the finishing stitch that pulls the pieces of the bag together.

1. Thread the sewing machine with thread in the desired color.

2. Place the finished edge to be topstitched under the presser foot with the right side facing up. Use the edge of the foot, or one of the seam allowance lines, as your guide to make sure the stitching is even.

Note: Go slowly and with a steady hand, since this stitching will be visible when the bag is complete.

APPLYING FUSIBLE INTERFACING

As you read through this book, you'll see that almost every pattern calls for interfacing. Interfacing is a strengthening material applied to the wrong side of the fabric to give the bag more structure. Fusible interfacing, which has heat-activated adhesive on one side, is affixed to a piece of fabric using the heat and moderate pressure of an iron. For the projects in this book, interfacing with a 45" (114cm) width is used to be sure all pieces could be cut from the same sheet.

1. Cut the interfacing, following the pattern specifications.

2. Place the adhesive side of the interfacing on the wrong side of the fabric.

3. Set an iron to medium heat with the steam function activated. To fuse, hold the iron down firmly on the uncoated side

of the interfacing for 10 to 15 seconds. Lift and, overlapping the spot you just ironed slightly, continue pressing the entire piece. It is important to remember not to slide the iron, but pick it up and move it in just one direction across the interfacing.

4. Iron the fabric on the right side to remove any excess moisture or air pockets.

INSERTING ZIPPERS

Often considered a daunting task, putting a zipper in your bag is a cinch if you insert it while the bag is still flat and in-progress. Here are the steps for inserting a zipper into just about any bag.

1. Start by ironing the fabric portion of the zipper flat.

2. Fuse narrow strips of Wonder Under, a web adhesive available at craft stores, to the right side of each side of the zipper tape, close to the outer edge. Remove the paper backing from the fusible web strips.

3. Position the right side of the zipper on the wrong side of the fabric to which you are attaching it, and press with an iron so the zipper adheres to the fabric.

4. Sew along each side and across the bottom of the zipper to secure it in place. Use caution when sewing over zipper teeth. **Please note:** Zippers will usually stick out past both ends of a piece of fabric initially.

CREATING GUSSETS

Gussets are the usually diamond-shaped or triangular inserts at the seams of the lower left and right-hand corners of some bag styles. Gussets are what create the flat bottom of the bag.

1. With the bag piece inside out, pinch one of the bottom corners to create a triangle. Take a peak inside to make sure the side seam and the bottom seam are lining up in the corner on the right side.

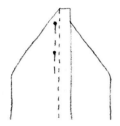

2. When the seams are aligned, secure the triangle on the outside with straight pins to the right or left of the middle seam, as shown in the diagram.

3. Repeat steps 1 and 2 on the other bottom corner.

4. Decide how large you want the gusset to be. With tailor's chalk, draw a horizontal line as long as the desired gusset with a ruler across the triangle you pinned. For example, if you'd like a 3" (7.5cm) gusset, place the ruler horizontally far enough from the tip of the triangle that the distance from the left-hand side to the right-hand side is 3" (7.5cm). Draw this line directly onto the bag fabric. Repeat this for the other corner as well.

5. Sew across both these lines. Turn the bag right side out.

GATHERING FABRIC WITH ELASTIC

Gathering fabric with elastic is an easy way to create even gathers on any bag. There is no pinning and no need to remove the elastic after the bag is sewn, since it adds no bulk to the seam.

1. Cut an unstretched length of elastic to the length you want the fabric gathering.

2. With tailor's chalk, draw lines to divide the elastic into quarters, and draw lines to divide the fabric edge to be gathered into quarters.

3. Place the elastic, parallel and ¼" (6mm) from fabric edge that is to be gathered. Anchor the end of the elastic with a few stitches.

4. Sew down the length of the elastic, stretching it as you sew to match the marks for each quarter.

ATTACHING BAG FEET

Bag feet are essential for protecting the bottom of your bags from dirt, moisture, and scrapes. Bag feet require no sewing or gluing, and they're a snap to apply. The only materials required are the bag feet, scissors, and plastic canvas. Plastic canvas is typically used for yarn projects and can be found in most craft supply stores.

1. With a pen, draw four dots in the corners of the flat bottom of the outside fabric piece. Each dot should be ½" (13mm) from each side. See diagram below for placement.

2. Using scissors, make tiny snips, slightly to the left and right of the dots you just made. Place the prongs on the bag feet through the holes.

3. Place the plastic canvas pieces inside the bottom of the exterior fabric piece to which you are attaching the bag feet, putting the prongs of the bag feet through the holes in the plastic canvas. The plastic canvas should lay flat on the bottom of the bag.

4. Spread out the prongs of the bag feet to secure them, as well as securing the canvas in the bottom of the bag.

CREATING ROUNDED BAG SHAPES

Not every bag needs to have squared off corners to be stylish. Rounded edges are easy to create, and add unique lines to any bag.

1. Find a household item such as a bowl or dish that has a diameter slightly wider than the pattern for the bag you are making. Place the bottom edge of the bowl so that it lines up with the bottom edge of the wrong side of the bag fabric.

2. Trace the rounded edge of the bowl onto the fabric.

3. Stitch along this line when joining the two sides of the bag to create the rounded shape.

SEWING ZIPPERED POCKETS

While this technique may sound difficult, this simple explanation will make adding zippered pockets to any bag a breeze. First, determine the finished size of the zippered pocket you'd like to create. Next, add 1" (2.5cm) to the width of the finished pocket dimensions. Double the height of the finished pocket dimensions and add 1" (2.5cm). For example, if you'd like to create a zipper pocket that is 6" (15cm) square, cut your fabric to 7" (18cm) wide x 13" (33cm) high.

1. Cut the piece of fabric to be used for the pocket based on formula above.

2. Find the center of the pocket piece. Following the example above, this would be 6½" (16.5cm) from the top and 3½" (9cm) from the left side. With the wrong side up, place the center of the pocket over the spot on the bag piece where you'd like to insert the zippered pocket. Secure it to the bag piece with straight pins.

3. On the spot where you'd like to insert your zipper, draw a rectangle on the wrong side of the pocket piece that is ½" (13mm) high and as wide as the zipper pocket, in this case 6" (15cm).

4. Stitch over the lines of the rectangle you just drew.

5. Cut a line in the middle of the rectangle that ends ½" (13mm) from each side. At ½" (13mm) from each end, cut diagonal lines into the corners.

6. Push the pocket though the window to the lining side.

7. To insert the zipper, start by ironing the fabric portion of the zipper flat. Fuse narrow strips of Wonder Under to the right side of each side of the zipper tape, close to the outer edge. Remove the paper backing from the Wonder Under.

8. Position the zipper onto the back of the fabric rectangle you just created. Press with an iron so the zipper adheres to the fabric box.

9. Sew along each side of the rectangle, catching the zipper tape in the stitching, to attach the zipper to the fabric rectangle.

10. On the wrong side of the bag piece where pocket has just been attached, bring the pocket sides together. Stitch around the sides and the bottom of the pocket.

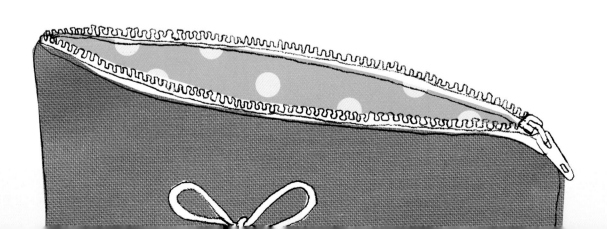

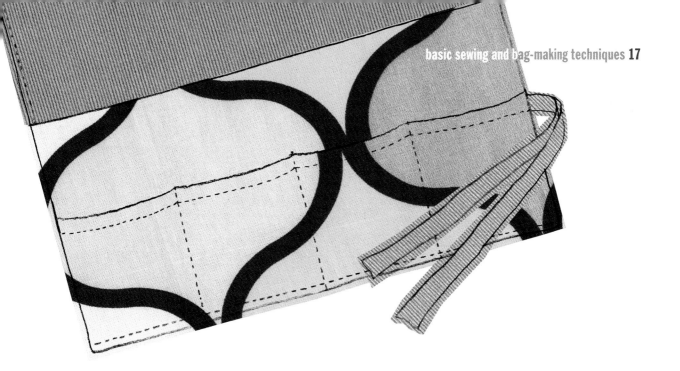

SEWING OPEN POCKETS

An open pocket is an uncomplicated way to add pockets to any project. First, determine the finished size of the open pocket you'd like to create. Next, add 1" (2.5cm) to the height of the finished pocket dimensions. Double the width of the finished pocket dimensions, and add 1" (2.5cm). For example, if you'd like to create an open pocket that is 6" (15cm) square, cut the fabric 7" (18cm) high x 13" (33cm) wide.

1. Cut the pocket fabric to the desired size, using the dimensions given above as a guideline.

2. Fold the pocket fabric in half crosswise, with the right sides of the fabric facing each other. Secure it with straight pins.

3. Stitch the open side and the bottom of the pocket using a ¼" (6mm) seam allowance. Turn the pocket right side out.

4. Fold the raw edge around the opening in ¾" (2cm) and secure it with straight pins.

5. Pin the pocket piece to the main bag fabric, so the raw edge is the bottom of the pocket.

6. Starting in the top right-hand corner and using a ¼" (6mm) seam allowance, stitch the pocket to the main bag fabric along the right-hand side, along the open bottom, and up the left-hand side to finish in the top left-hand corner.

CREATING CUSTOM BAG STRAPS FROM FABRIC

When you're creating different-sized bags, you'll need straps of different lengths and widths. First, determine the finished length of the strap you want to make. The pattern should always be 2" (5cm) longer than the desired finishing length. The extra 2" (5cm) will be used to attach the strap(s) to the bag. Now, determine the finished width of the strap. Take this width, double it, and add 2" (5cm). For example, to create a strap that is 30" (76cm) long and 1½" (3.8cm) wide, cut a piece of fabric that is 32" (81cm) long x 5" (12.5cm) wide.

1. Cut a piece of fabric and a piece of fusible interfacing to the strap pattern specifications, using the dimensions given above as a guideline. Fuse the interfacing to the wrong side of the strap.

2. Fold the raw edges on each side of this piece in 1" (2.5cm), as shown in the diagram.

3. Fold the strap piece in half lengthwise. To follow the example above, this creates a 1½" (3.8cm) wide strap. Secure with straight pins.

4. With a ⅛" (3mm) seam allowance, stitch along each side. Keep the stitches straight and neat, as shown in the diagram below.

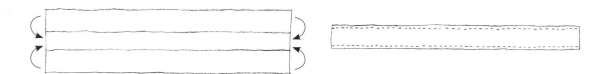

CREATING ADJUSTABLE STRAPS FROM NYLON WEBBING AND HARDWARE

You can create your own adjustable straps from nylon webbing, a metal slider, and two metal swivel hooks.

1. Determine the desired length for the adjustable strap. Keep in mind that the fully extended length has to be double the length of the strap when adjusted to its shortest. For example, an adjustable strap that is 25" (63.5cm) at its shortest length is 50" (127cm) at its longest length.

2. No matter what strap measurement you are creating, add an extra 8" (20.5cm) to the longest desired length of the adjustable strap for seam allowance. In the case of the example above, cut a piece of nylon webbing that is 58" (147.5cm) long.

3. Wrap one end of the nylon webbing strap through the ring of one of the metal swivel hooks. There should be 2" of strap overhang. Fold over 1" (2.5cm) and secure it to the rest of the strap with a straight pin. Create a ⅞" (2.2cm) box stitch on the end of the strap to secure the overhang to rest of strap.

4. Slide on the metal slider.

5. Slide on the other metal swivel hook to the halfway point on the nylon webbing piece.

6. Slide the other end of the nylon webbing through the metal slider so there is a 2" (5cm) overhang. Fold over 1" (2.5cm) of the webbing, and secure to the rest of the strap with a straight pin. Create a ⅞" (2.2cm) box stitch on the end of the strap securing the overhang to rest of strap.

INSERTING MAGNETIC SNAPS

Inserting magnetic snaps into a bag is simple and a great way to keep your bag closed without a fussy zipper.

1. Mark the areas where you want place each snap. Reinforce the wrong side of the fabric where you're going to apply the snaps with a small square of fusible interfacing.

2. Make two very small slits, one slightly to the left of your marking and one slightly to the right. (A seam ripper is perfect for this job.)

3. Push the prongs of one half of the snap into the right side of the fabric.

4. Slip one of the thin metal disks that came with the snap over the prongs on the wrong side of the snap, and then push the prongs down flat (away from each other) with your thumb.

5. Repeat Steps 2–5 for the other half of the snap.

handbags and purses

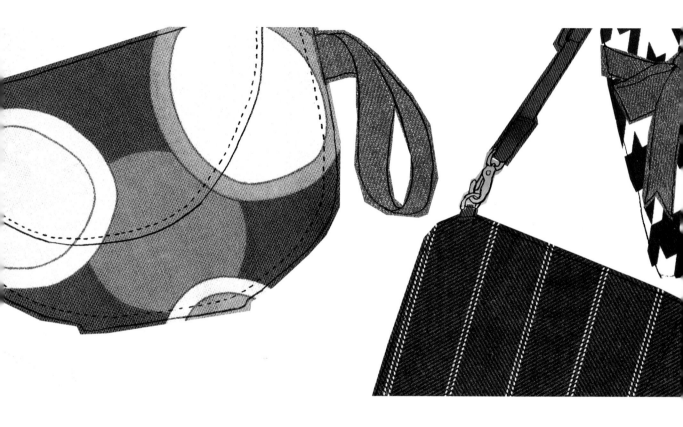

what you need:

1 yd (91cm) heavy fusible interfacing   •   ½ yd (45.5cm) printed tweed fabric (or any heavy cotton fabric)   •   Posterboard or large folder for pattern   •   ½ yd (45.5cm) matching satin fabric for lining   •   16mm magnetic snap   •   1½ yd (1.4m) matching grosgrain ribbon   •   Scissors   •   Iron and ironing board   •   Sewing machine   •   Matching color thread   •   Straight pins

Dressed up or down, flashy or simple, this chic shoulder bag has all the room you need for toting your everyday essentials. The simple shape can accommodate a variety of fun, funky, or classic fabrics, and the grosgrain ribbon accent pulls the whole look together.

ALICE SHOULDER BAG

PREP WORK

1. Cut out 1 piece of fusible interfacing and 1 piece of the tweed fabric, measuring 28" (71cm) long x 5" (12.5cm) wide for the strap.

2. Fold and sew the strap piece into a 1½" (3.8cm) wide strap, referring to "Creating Custom Bag Straps from Fabric" (page 18).

3. Create a pattern for the main piece, based on the dimensions shown below. You can create the pattern out of posterboard or a large heavyweight folder.

4. Trace the main pattern piece onto fusible interfacing 4 times and cut out each one.

5. Place 2 fusible interfacing pieces, with the shiny glue side down, on the wrong side of the tweed fabric. Press with an iron so the entire piece of interfacing fuses to the fabric.

6. Place 2 pieces of fusible interfacing, with the shiny glue side down, on the wrong side of the lining fabric. Press with an iron so the entire piece of interfacing fuses to the fabric.

7. Cut out both pieces of the tweed and lining fabrics, using the edge of the interfacing pieces as a guide for where to cut.

ASSEMBLY

1. With right sides together, pin both tweed pieces together. With a ¼" (6mm) seam allowance, sew the tweed pieces together along both sides and the bottom, leaving the top open as shown in Diagram 1.

2. Repeat step 1, using the lining pieces.

3. Create 3" gussets (page 14) in the bottom corners of both the tweed and lining pieces.

4. Turn the tweed pieces right side out, and place the lining inside the tweed.

5. Fold in the top edge of the tweed ¾" (2cm) to the wrong side. This will eliminate the raw edge. Secure the fold with straight pins.

6. Fold in the top edge of the lining ¾" (2cm) to the wrong side

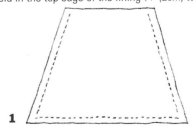

skill level: Easy   **pattern dimensions:** 11" (28cm) wide at the top • 16" (40.5cm) wide at the bottom x 12" (30.5cm) high

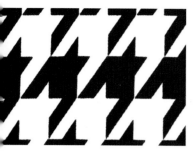

ALICE SHOULDER BAG

so the top edge aligns with the top edge of the exterior fabric. Secure with the same straight pins used on the tweed.

7. Insert one raw end of the strap 1" (2.5cm) into the side of the bag, between the tweed and the lining, aligning the center of the strap with the side seam. Secure with a straight pin. Insert the other raw end of the strap 1" (2.5cm) into the other side of the bag, between the tweed and the lining, aligning the center of the strap with the side seam.

8. Make a mark with a pen on the inside of the lining, an equal distance from each side seam, 2" (5cm) from the top edge on both the front and back. Insert the magnetic snap at this mark (page 19).

9. Topstitch ¼" (6mm) from the top edge of the bag, making sure to catch the strap ends, until you return to the point where you started (page 12).

10. Wrap the 1½ yd (1.4m) of matching grosgrain ribbon around the top of the bag 2" (5cm) down from the top, and tie in a bow. Slide the bow to either the center or to the left or right of center (as desired) and secure it with straight pins.

11. With matching thread, neatly hand-stitch the ribbon to each side seam of the bag.

12. Remove all pins and trim all loose threads.

Resembling a traditional bike messenger bag, the Mia has plenty of room inside, with three compartments, an adjustable strap, and a full-size flap closure with a magnetic snap.

MIA MESSENGER BAG

what you need:

Posterboard or large folder for pattern • 2 yd (1.8m) heavyweight fusible interfacing • 1 yd (91cm) heavy cotton fabric for lining • ¾ yd (69cm) printed canvas fabric (or any heavy cotton fabric) • 4 bag feet • 1 piece of plastic canvas measuring 3" (7.5cm) x 10" (25cm) long. • One 18" (45.5cm) dress zipper • 16mm magnetic snap • 1¾ yd (1.6m) x 2" (5cm) nylon webbing • Two 2" (5cm) metal rings • Two 2" (5cm) metal spring hooks for strap • One 2" (5cm) metal slider for strap • Scissors • Ruler • Pen • Iron and ironing board • Straight pins • Sewing machine • Matching color thread

MIA MESSENGER BAG

PREP WORK

1. Create patterns for the main piece, the flap piece, and the divider based on the dimensions below. You can create the patterns out of posterboard or a large folder.

2. Trace 4 of the main pattern pieces onto fusible interfacing, and cut them out.

3. Trace 2 of the flap pattern pieces onto fusible interfacing, and cut them out.

4. Trace 4 of the divider pattern pieces directly onto the heavy cotton lining fabric, and cut them out.

5. Place 2 of the main fusible interfacing pieces, with shiny glue side down, on the wrong side of the printed canvas making sure the print of the fabric is facing the correct way. Press with an iron so the entire piece of interfacing fuses to the fabric (page 13).

6. Place the 2 remaining main fusible interfacing pieces, with shiny glue side down, on the wrong side of the lining fabric. Press with an iron so the entire piece of interfacing fuses to the fabric.

7. Place 1 of the fusible interfacing flap pieces, with the shiny glue side down, on the wrong side of the canvas. Press with an iron so the entire piece of interfacing fuses to the fabric.

8. Place the other fusible interfacing flap piece, with the shiny glue side down, on the wrong side of the lining. Press with an iron so the entire piece of interfacing fuses to the fabric.

9. Cut out all fused fabric pieces, using the edge of the interfacing as a guide for where to cut.

skill level: Intermediate

pattern dimensions: Main: 14" (35.5cm) x 14" (35.5cm) • Flap: 12" (30.5cm) x 11" (28cm) • Divider: 11" (28cm) x 11" (28cm)

ASSEMBLY

1. With right sides together, pin the main canvas pieces together. With a ¼" (6mm) seam allowance, sew the 2 pieces together along both sides and the bottom, leaving the top open as shown in Diagram 1.

2. Create 3" (7.5cm) gussets (page 14) in the bottom corners of the canvas pieces.

3. Insert 1 bag foot (page 15) into each corner of the exterior fabric piece.

4. With right sides together, line up the edge of the zipper with the top edge of one of the divider pieces, and secure with straight pins, as shown in Diagram 2.

5. With a ⅛" (3mm) seam allowance, sew the edge of the zipper (page 13) to the top edge of the divider piece.

6. With right sides together, line up another piece of the divider with the other side of the zipper. Make sure the edge of the zipper and the top edge of the fabric piece line up; the zipper will be hidden between the 2 layers of fabric. Secure with straight pins.

7. Sew the divider piece to the zipper.

8. Turn this piece right side out, so the zipper is sticking out between the 2 layers of divider pieces (Diagram 3).

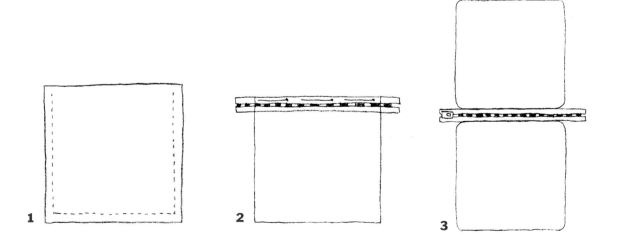

1

2

3

MIA MESSENGER BAG

9. Flip the divider piece open, so the zipper is in the middle and the 2 divider pieces are on either side of the zipper.

10. Topstitch (page 12) along each side of the zipper ¼" (6mm) from the zipper teeth, as shown in Diagram 4.

11. Fold the divider piece in half so the zipper is at the top and the raw edges are at the bottom.

12. Place the right sides of the left-hand side of the divider piece and the left-hand piece of the main lining fabric together, with the zipper portion of the divider about 2" (5cm) below the top edge of the main lining piece. Secure it with straight pins.

13. With a ¼" (6mm) seam allowance, stitch securely along this left-hand edge.

14. Place the right sides of the right-hand side of the divider piece and the right-hand piece of the main lining together, with that the zipper portion of the divider about 2" (5cm) below the top edge of the main lining piece.

15. With a ¼" (6mm) seam allowance, stitch securely along this right-hand edge.

16. With right sides together, place the remaining lining piece on top of the sewn lining and divider piece. Secure with straight pins in each corner.

17. With a ¼" (6mm) seam allowance, stitch the lining pieces together along the right- and left-hand sides, following the stitching from steps 13 and 15, when the divider was attached to the the lining.

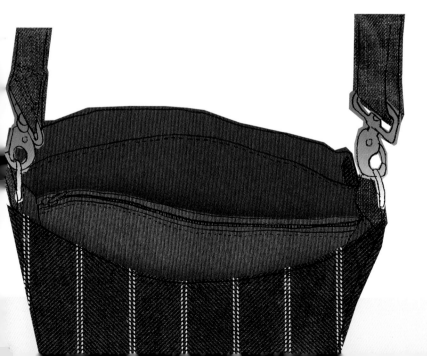

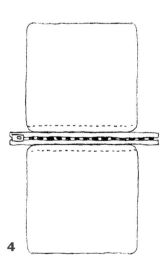

4

18. With a ¼" (6mm) seam allowance, stitch along the bottom, making sure to catch the bottom of the divider piece in between the layers of the lining. Start and stop stitching 2" (5cm) from the corners.

19. Create 3" (7.5cm) gussets in the bottom corners of the lining piece.

20. Turn the canvas piece right side out, and place the lining piece inside.

21. Fold in the top edge of the canvas ¾" (2cm). This will eliminate the raw edge. Secure with straight pins.

22. Fold out the top edge of the lining ¾" (2cm) so it lines with the top edge of the canvas. Secure with the same straight pins used on the exterior fabric, as shown in Diagram 5.

23. With right sides together, pin the canvas flap piece to the flap lining. With a ¼" (6mm) seam allowance, sew the 2 fabric pieces together along both 12" (30.5cm) sides and the bottom 11" (28cm) side, as shown in Diagram 6. Turn the flap piece right side out.

24. Topstitch ¼" (6mm) from the edge around the same 3 sides of the flap you have just sewn.

25. Make a mark with a pen an equal distance from each edge of the flap piece, on the lining side, 2" (5cm) from the bottom, topstitched edge.

5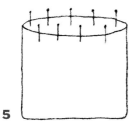

6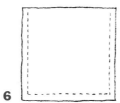

MIA MESSENGER BAG

Insert the "outie" part of the magnetic snap here (page 19).

26. Tuck the raw edge of the flap in between the outside and the lining pieces of the main bag pieces 1" (2.5cm) from the edge, and secure it with straight pins, as shown in Diagram 7.

27. Fold the flap down, as if you were closing the bag. Make a mark in pen where the "outie" part of the snap hits the canvas on the main part of the bag. Insert the "innie" side of the magnetic snap here.

28. Cut two 4" (10cm) lengths of nylon webbing.

29. Wrap each 4" (10cm) long piece of webbing around each of the 2" (5cm) rings and pin the ends together as shown in Diagram 8.

30. With a ¼" (6mm) seam allowance, stitch across the bottom edge of the webbing wrapped around the ring.

31. Tuck the stitched edge of the webbing (attached to the ring) down 1" (2.5cm) in between the canvas and the lining of the main bag. The center of each length of webbing should be lined up with the side seams.

32. With a ¼" (6mm) seam allowance, topstitch all the way around the top edge of the bag, making sure to catch the flap and webbing pieces you pinned in the last steps.

33. Create an adjustable strap (page 19) that measures 25" (63.5cm) at the shortest length and 50" (127cm) at the longest length.

34. Clip the strap to the rings on the sides of the bag.

35. Remove all pins and trim all loose threads.

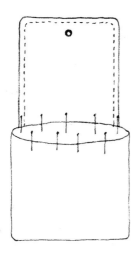

7

8

The flap closure on this versatile backpack provides easy access to the spacious inner compartment. With loads of room for books and magazines, as well as a handy zipper pocket inside for storing smaller items, this bag is perfect for work, school, or play.

LAUREN BACKPACK

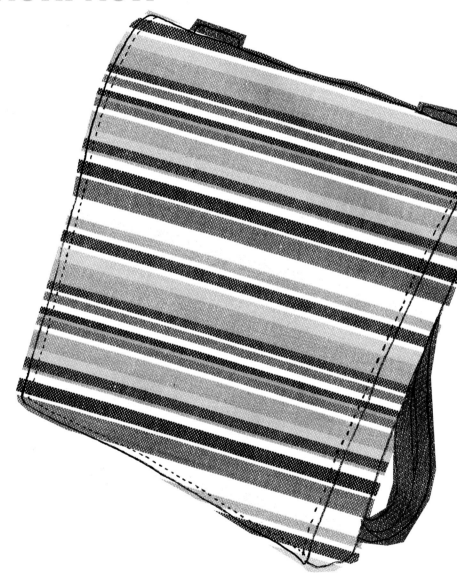

what you need:

Posterboard or large folder for pattern • 2 yd (1.8m) heavy fusible interfacing • 1½ yd (1.4m) heavy canvas (or denim) fabric • 1½ yd (1.4m) matching broadcloth lining fabric • 3 yd (2.75m) x 1½" (3.8cm) nylon webbing • Four 2" (3.8cm) metal rings • One 8" (20.5cm) dress zipper (to canvas or denim fabric) • One 20" (51cm) dress zipper (to match canvas fabric) • 16mm magnetic snap • Four 1½" (3.8cm) metal spring hooks for straps • Two 1½" (3.8cm) metal sliders for straps • Scissors • Sewing machine • Iron and ironing board • Straight pins • Matching color thread

LAUREN BACKPACK

PREP WORK

1. Create patterns for the main piece, the pocket, and the flap pieces, based on the dimensions below. You can create the patterns out of posterboard or a large folder.

2. Trace 4 of the main pattern pieces onto fusible interfacing, and cut them out.

3. Trace 2 of the flap pattern pieces onto fusible interfacing, and cut them out.

4. Trace 1 of the pocket pattern pieces onto fusible interfacing, and cut it out.

5. Place 2 of the main fusible interfacing pieces, with the shiny glue side down, on the wrong side of the heavy canvas or denim. Press with an iron so the entire piece of interfacing fuses to the fabric (page 13).

6. Place the 2 remaining main fusible interfacing pieces, with the shiny glue side down, on the wrong side of the lining fabric. Press with an iron so the entire piece of interfacing fuses to the fabric.

7. Place one of the fusible interfacing flap pieces, with the shiny glue side down, on the wrong side of the canvas. Press with an iron so the entire piece of interfacing fuses to the fabric.

8. Place the remaining fusible interfacing flap piece, with the shiny glue side down, on the wrong side of the lining fabric.

Press with an iron so the entire piece of interfacing fuses to the fabric.

9. Place the pocket interfacing piece, with the shiny glue side down, on the wrong side of the canvas. Press with an iron so the entire piece of interfacing fuses to the fabric.

10. Cut out all fabric pieces, using the edge of the interfacing pieces as guides for where to cut.

11. Trace the pocket pattern piece directly onto the wrong side of the lining fabric and cut it out.

12. Cut out a 7" (18cm) x 13" (33cm) piece of the lining fabric to be used for the additional inside zipper pocket.

13. Cut the nylon webbing into three 1-yd (91cm) pieces. Cut one of the 1-yd (91cm) pieces into four 8" (20.5cm) pieces. (Discard the extra 4" [10cm] piece.)

14. Wrap each 8" (20.5cm) length of webbing around each of the 2" (5cm) rings and pin the ends together, as shown in Diagram 1.

1

skill level: Intermediate

pattern dimensions: Main: 20" (51cm) x 18" (45.5cm) • Flap: 20" (51cm) x 15" (38cm) • Pocket: 16" (40.5cm) x 18" (45.5cm)

LAUREN BACKPACK

ASSEMBLY

1. With right sides together, stitch together the canvas pocket piece and the lining fabric pocket pieces along 3 sides, leaving the bottom open. Turn the pocket right side out. Fold the raw fabric edge down. With right sides together, pin the edge of the zipper to the folded top edge of the pocket. Secure with straight pins.

2. With a ⅛" (3mm) seam allowance, stitch the edge of the zipper to the folded edge of the pocket.

3. With right sides together, place the pocket piece on top of one of the main canvas pieces. Line up the bottoms of both the main piece and the pocket piece. The zipper on the pocket should fall 5" (12.5cm) from the top of the piece of canvas.

4. With a ⅛" (3mm) seam allowance, stitch the pocket piece to the main canvas piece along the two sides and the bottom.

5. With right sides together, pin the remaining canvas piece to the canvas piece with the pocket attached. Pin the webbing portion of 2 of the webbing/ring combinations in between the canvas pieces at the bottom, so the end with the ring is in between the fabric layers and the raw end of the webbing is sticking out approximately 1" (2.5cm). Each webbing and ring should be 3" (7.5cm) from each bottom corner. Secure with straight pins.

6. With a ¼" (6mm) seam allowance, sew both canvas pieces together along the sides and bottom, leaving the top open, as shown in Diagram 2, and making sure to catch the webbing pinned in step 5.

7. Insert an additional 6" (15cm) x 6" (15cm) zipper pocket (page 16) into the top portion of 1 of your main lining pieces.

8. Repeat step 5 with the lining pieces, excluding the nylon webbing and rings.

9. Create 2" (5cm) gussets (page 14) in the bottom corners of both the canvas and lining pieces.

10. Turn the canvas piece right side out, then place the lining inside the canvas.

11. Fold the top edge of the canvas in ¾" (2cm). This will eliminate the raw edge. Secure with straight pins.

12. Fold the top edge of the lining out ¾" (2cm) so the top edge matches the top edge of the outside fabric. Secure with same straight pins used on the canvas in step 10.

13. With right sides together, pin the canvas flap piece to the flap lining. Using a ¼" (6mm) seam allowance, sew the two fabric pieces together along both 20" (51cm) sides and the bottom 15" (38cm) side.

14. Turn the flap piece right side out. Topstitch ¼" (6mm) from the edge around the same three sides of the flap you have just sewn (page 12).

15. On the flap lining, make a mark in pen an equal distance from each side of the flap, 2" (5cm) from the bottom, topstitched edge. Insert the innie part of the magnetic snap here (page 19).

16. Tuck the raw edge of the flap down 1" (2.5cm) in between the canvas and lining pieces of the bag. Secure it with straight pins, as shown in Diagram 3.

17. Tuck the stitched edge of the two remaining webbing ring pieces 3" (7.5cm) from each side seam, in between the outside and the flap layers of the back of the bag.

18. Topstitch ¼" (6mm) from the top edge all the way around the top edge of the bag, making sure to catch the flap and the webbing pieces you pinned in the previous steps.

19. From the remaining two 1-yd (91cm) pieces of nylon webbing, create 2 adjustable straps (page 19) that measure 15" (38cm) at shortest length and 30" (76cm) at longest length.

20. Clip the ends of the straps to the 4 rings on the top and bottom of the bag.

21. Remove all pins and trim all loose threads.

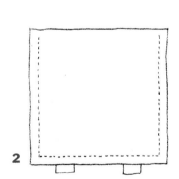

2

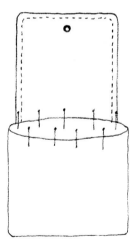

3

what you need:

Posterboard or large folder to create pattern • ½ yd (45.5cm) heavy fusible interfacing • ¼ yd (23cm) silk or satin fabric
• ¼ yd (23cm) matching satin fabric for lining • 14mm magnetic snap • Scissors • Sewing machine • Iron and ironing board
• Straight pins • Matching color thread

This simple, envelope-style clutch is the perfect mini-accessory for an evening on the town.

HEATHER ENVELOPE-STYLE EVENING CLUTCH

PREP WORK

1. Create a pattern for the main piece, cut to the dimensions below. You can create the pattern out of posterboard or a large folder.

2. Trace 2 of the main pattern pieces onto fusible interfacing and cut them out.

3. With the shiny glue side down, place 1 of the fusible interfacing pieces onto the wrong side of the exterior fabric. Place the other piece of interfacing onto the lining fabric. Press with an iron so each piece of interfacing fuses to the fabrics.

4. Cut out both the exterior and lining pieces, using the edge of the interfacing as a guide for where to cut.

5. With right sides together, pin both pieces together along the stitch lines shown in Diagram 1.

ASSEMBLY

1. With a ¼" (6mm) seam allowance, sew the outside fabric piece to the lining piece, along all edges except the bottom, as shown in Diagram 1.

2. Turn the clutch right side out, making sure to really poke out the corners. Chopsticks can be particularly handy for this. You want them to be squared off, rather than looking rounded.

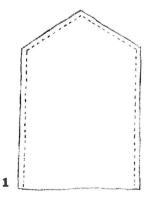

1

skill level: Easy　　**pattern dimensions:** Main: 15" (38cm) x 11" (28cm)

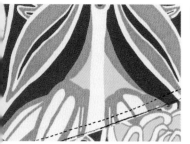

HEATHER ENVELOPE-STYLE CLUTCH

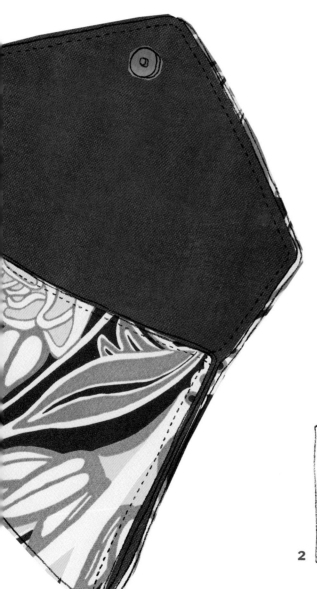

3. Make a pen mark at the top of your clutch piece on the lining fabric, 1" (2.5cm) down from the top of the point. Insert the outie side of the magnetic snap here (page 19).

4. Fold the bottom open edge of the clutch in ¾" (2cm). This will eliminate the raw fabric edges and create a clean, straight line on the bottom of the clutch piece. Once the line is straight, secure it with straight pins, as shown in Diagram 2.

5. Fold the bottom portion of the clutch piece as far up as you would like the pocket to extend. This should be at least ⅓ the height of the whole piece. Fold more for a larger pocket and smaller flap (see Diagram 3). In the example below, the pocket piece is folded up approximately 4" (10cm).

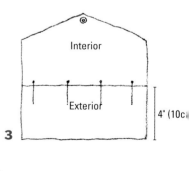

Interior

Exterior

4" (10c

3

Interior

2 ←— Fold line

6. Fold the flap down and make a pen mark where the outie part of the snap hits the exterior fabric. Insert the innie part of the magnetic snap. Unfold the flap as well as the bottom pocket portion of the bag.

7. Topstitch ¼" (6mm) from the pinned open edge (page 12).

8. Refold the bottom pocket portion of the clutch and neatly topstitch, starting at the right bottom folded edge and continue around the outside of the bag except for the bottom folded edge, as shown in Diagram 4.

9. Remove all pins and trim all loose threads.

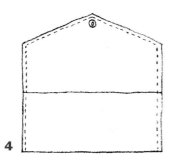

4

what you need:

Posterboard or large folder for patterns • ½ yd (45.5cm) fusible interfacing • ½ yd (45.5cm) silk or satin fabric
• ½ yd (45.5cm) matching satin fabric for lining • Purse frame • Scissors • Iron and ironing board • Sewing machine
• Straight pins • Matching color thread • Tailor's chalk

The hardware incorporated in this design not only adds style and class to this evening bag, it also allows easy access to your evening essentials.

WENDY FRAME-STYLE CLUTCH

PREP WORK

1. Create a pattern for the main piece, based on the dimensions below. You can create the patterns out of posterboard or a large folder.

2. Trace 4 copies of the pattern onto the fusible interfacing, and cut out.

3. With the shiny glue side down, place 2 pieces of interfacing onto the wrong side of the exterior fabric and 2 pieces onto the wrong side of the lining fabric. Press with an iron so the entire piece of interfacing fuses to the fabrics (page 13).

4. Cut out both fabric pieces, using the edge of the interfacing as a guide for where to cut.

ASSEMBLY

1. With right sides together, pin the top of 1 piece of exterior fabric to 1 piece of lining fabric. Pin the remaining exterior fabric piece to the remaining lining fabric piece the same way.

2. With a ¼" (6mm) seam allowance, stitch the top (shorter side) of the exterior fabric to the top of the lining for both pieces pinned in prior step.

3. Open up each piece you just stitched, so both the exterior fabric and the lining on both pieces are right side up.

4. With right sides together, pin these pieces together along the bottom edge of the exterior pieces so the exterior and lining pieces line up. The stitch lines you created in step 2 should also be aligned. See Diagram 1 below.

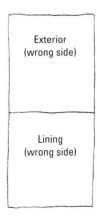

Exterior (wrong side)

Lining (wrong side)

1

skill level: Intermediate   **pattern dimensions:** Main: 11"W (28cm) x 8½"T (21.5cm)

WENDY FRAME-STYLE CLUTCH

5. Using tailor's chalk, make 4 marks on 1 of the wrong sides of the fabric: Mark 1" (2.5cm) from each outer edge and 2" (5cm) from the middle seam line on both the exterior fabric and the lining fabric. See Diagram 2.

6. With a ¼" (6mm) seam allowance, stitch the 2 pieces together, starting at the top right-hand corner mark on the lining. Continue down the right-hand side, across the bottom (short side), and back up the left-hand side of the lining to the mark on the left-hand corner. Continue stitching from the bottom left mark on the exterior fabric around to the last mark. **Do not stitch between the star marks** (see Diagram 3).

7. Turn the entire piece right side out. Fold the raw fabric edges in ¼" (6mm) on both of the areas not sewn in the last step. Secure with straight pins.

8. Using ¼" seam allowance, stitch the fabric folded in the last step. Repeat for both the left- and the right-hand sides.

9. Turn inside out again, and create 2" (5cm) gussets in the bottom corners of both the exterior fabric and the lining (page 14).

10. Turn the entire piece right side out.

11. Stuff the lining portion of the bag inside the exterior portion, making sure the stitched top edge of both the exterior fabric and the lining is even.

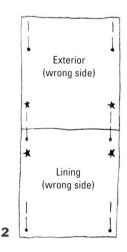

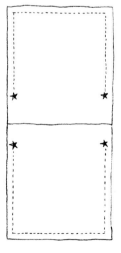

Exterior
(wrong side)

Lining
(wrong side)

2

3

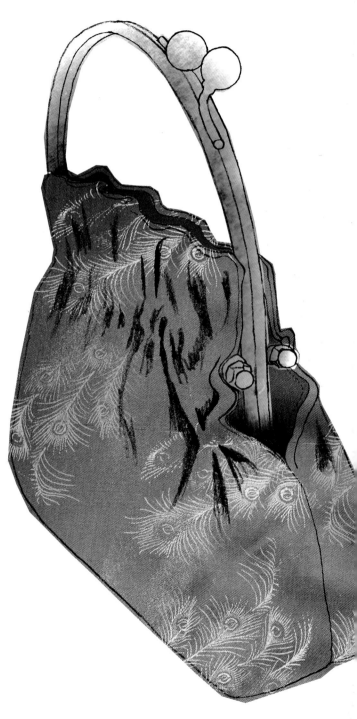

12. With tailor's chalk, draw a line around the lining at the point where the hole in each side seam begins, about 2" (5cm) from the top of the bag. Draw another line ½" (13mm) above the first line.

13. Topstitch all the way around the bag along both of these lines. See Diagram 4.

14. Insert the rods of the purse frame into the channels you created in the last step. Secure the frame into the purse fabric by screwing the end knobs onto the frame rods.

15. Trim all loose threads.

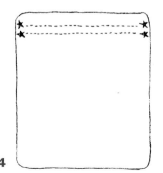

4

MELISSA WRISTLET

what you need:

½ yd (45.5cm) silk or satin fabric (something a little dressy) for exterior • Posterboard or large folder for patterns • ½ yd (45.5cm) fusible interfacing • ½ yd (45.5cm) matching satin lining fabric • 7" (18cm) zipper • Scissors • Iron and ironing board • Sewing machine • Straight pins • Matching color thread

This simple wristlet leaves your hands free while it keeps your essentials for an evening out close by.

PREP WORK

1. Cut out a 12" (30cm) x 4" (10cm) piece of the exterior fabric. This piece will be used for the wristlet strap.

2. Fold in each side and sew this piece into a 1" (2.5cm) wide strap (page 18).

3. Create a pattern for the main piece, based on the dimensions of page 44. You can create the patterns out of posterboard or a large folder.

4. Trace 4 copies of the above pattern onto the fusible interfacing, and cut them out.

5. Place 2 of the fusible interfacing pieces onto the wrong side of the exterior fabric.

6. Place the remaining 2 fusible interfacing pieces onto the wrong side of the lining fabric.

7. Press all 4 pieces with an iron so the entire piece of interfacing fuses to the fabric (page 13).

8. Cut out all fabric pieces, using the edge of the interfacing as a guide for where to cut.

ASSEMBLY

1. With right sides together, place the zipper flush with the top of 1 exterior fabric piece. Secure with straight pins.

2. With a ⅛" (3mm) seam allowance, stitch the top of the zipper to the top of the exterior fabric.

3. With right sides together, place 1 of the lining fabric pieces on top of the exterior piece with the zipper attached to it. The zipper should be between these 2 layers. Secure it with straight pins.

4. With a ⅛" (3mm) seam allowance, stitch the top of the lining fabric piece to the top of the exterior piece. Turn the bag right side out.

5. With right sides together, place the other side of the zipper flush with the top of the remaining exterior fabric piece. Secure it with straight pins as shown in Diagram 1 on page 46.

6. With a ⅛" (3mm) seam allowance, stitch the top of the zipper to the top of this exterior piece.

7. With right sides together, place the other piece of lining fabric on top of the second piece of exterior fabric. Again, the zipper should be between these 2 layers. Secure it with straight pins.

MELISSA EVENING WRISTLET

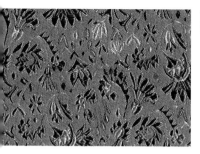

8. With a ⅛" (3mm) seam allowance, sew the top of the lining fabric to the top of the exterior fabric.

9. Pin the bag so the exterior fabric pieces are lined up with each other and the lining fabric pieces are lined up with each other. The zipper should be between them.

10. Open the zipper so the zipper pull is halfway between the right- and left-hand side.

11. Secure the open side of the zipper with a straight pin.

12. Place the wristlet strap in between the layers of exterior fabric, 1" (2.5cm) down from the zipper, so the raw edges of the wristlet strap are sticking out from the side approximately 1" (2.5cm), as shown in Diagram 2.

13. Starting at the lower left-hand corner, stitch all the way around 3 sides, leaving the bottom section open, as shown in Diagram 3. Be sure to backstitch a couple of times across where the raw edge of the strap is sticking out for added durability.

14. Open the zipper the rest of the way.

15. Turn the bag right side out, making sure to poke out the corners. You can use a chopstick for this. Corners should be squared, rather than rounded.

16. Fold in the bottom open edge of the lining fabric in ½" (13mm) all the way around to get rid of the raw fabric edges and create a straight line on the bottom of your bag. Secure with straight pins.

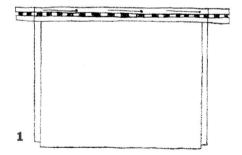

1

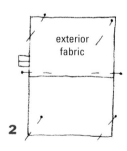

2

exterior fabric

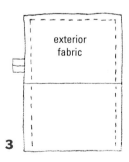

3

exterior fabric

skill level: Intermediate   **pattern dimensions:** 9" (23cm) x 6" (15cm)

17. Topstitch all the way across this edge ¼" (6mm) from the bottom.

18. Remove all pins and trim all loose threads.

19. Stuff the lining back into the outside of the bag. Make sure the lining is lying flat inside the bag.

what you need:

½ yd (45.5cm) heavy cotton print fabric • 1½ yd (1.4m) heavy fusible interfacing • Kate Hobo Bag template (page 124) • Posterboard or large folder for pattern • ½ yd (45.5cm) heavy canvas or vinyl solid fabric • ½ yd (45.5cm) matching satin lining fabric (C) • 18" (45.5cm) dress zipper • Two 2" (5cm) rings • Scissors • Sewing machine • Iron and ironing board • Straight pins • Matching thread

Kate resembles the traditional hobo style bag, but the overlapping complementary fabrics add depth and style to this unique purse.

KATE HOBO BAG

PREP WORK

1. Cut out a piece of printed outside fabric measuring 16" (40.5cm) x 5" (12.5cm) and a piece of fusible interfacing of the size. These pieces will be used for the strap.

2. Fold and sew one 1½" (3.8cm) wide strap (page 18).

3. Using the template on page 124, create a pattern for the pattern pieces, based on the dimensions and shapes shown below. You can create the pattern out of posterboard or a large folder.

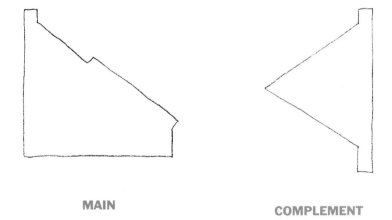

MAIN   COMPLEMENT

skill level: Advanced   **pattern dimensions:** Main: 18" (45.5cm) x 18" (45.5cm) •
Complement: 10" (25.5cm) x 18" (45.5cm) • Lining: 18" (45.5cm) x 18" (45.5cm)

KATE **HOBO BAG**

4. Trace 2 of the main pattern pieces onto fusible interfacing, and cut them out.

5. Trace 2 of the complementary pattern pieces onto fusible interfacing, and cut them out.

6. Trace 2 of the lining pattern pieces onto fusible interfacing, and cut them out.

7. Place 2 fusible interfacing main pieces, with the shiny glue side down, on the wrong side of the cotton print fabric. Press with an iron so the entire piece of interfacing fuses to the fabric (page 13).

8. Place 2 fusible interfacing complementary pieces, with the shiny glue side down, on the wrong side of the canvas or vinyl fabric. Press with an iron so the entire piece of interfacing fuses to the fabric.

9. Place 2 fusible interfacing lining pieces, with the shiny glue side down, on the wrong side of the satin lining fabric. Press with an iron so the entire piece of interfacing fuses to the fabric.

10. Cut out all fabric pieces using the edge of the interfacing as a guide for where to cut.

LINING

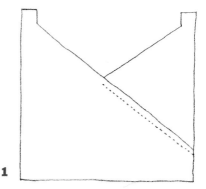

1

ASSEMBLY

1. Place one of the cotton print pieces on top of one of the canvas or vinyl solid pieces. Fold over the tab of cotton fabric that extends over the canvas or vinyl, and secure the pieces in place with straight pins.

2. Topstitch ¼" (6mm) from the edge along the cotton piece (page 12), sewing it to the canvas or vinyl piece, as shown in Diagram 1.

3. Repeat steps 1 and 2 with the remaining cotton and canvas or vinyl pieces.

4. With right sides together, place both of these outside pieces together and secure with straight pins.

5. With right sides together, place both lining pieces together and secure with straight pins.

6. Stitch along both sides and the bottom of the outside pieces and then the lining pieces, as shown Diagrams 2 and 3.

7. Create 3" (7.5cm) gussets in the bottom corners of both the outside fabric pieces and the lining fabric pieces. See "Creating Gussets" (page 14) for more information.

8. Turn the outside fabric piece right side out.

9. With right sides together, place 1 side of the zipper flush with the front of the outside fabric piece . Secure the zipper in place with straight pins.

10. Using ⅛" (3mm) seam allowance, stitch one side of the zipper to the front of the outside fabric piece.

11. With right sides together, place the other side of the zipper flush with the wrong side of the outside fabric piece. Secure it with straight pins.

12. Using ⅛" (3mm) seam allowance, stitch the other side of the zipper to the back of the outside fabric piece.

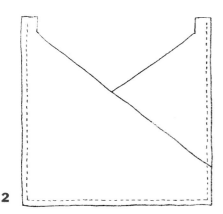

2

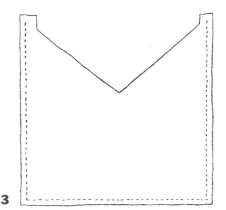

3

KATE **HOBO BAG**

13. Undo the zipper and drop the lining fabric piece into the outside fabric piece.

14. Turn the top layer of the lining fabric over ½" (13mm) to line up with the zippered edge of the outside fabric piece. Secure with straight pins.

15. Topstitch the top edge of the lining fabric to the outside fabric piece a ¼" (6mm) from the top.

16. Fold each tab at the top corners of the bag over one of the 2" (5cm) rings 1" (2.5cm) and secure them in place with straight pins.

17. Topstitch the top corner tabs to secure 1 side of the ring to the bag.

18. Fold 1 edge of the strap you created in steps 1 and 2 of the Prep Work over the other side of 1 of the 2" (5cm) rings, and secure it with a straight pin.

19. Topstitch to secure the other side of the ring to the strap. Repeat steps 17 and 18 with the other end of the strap.

20. Remove all pins and trim all loose threads.

Constructed with a fun and durable upholstery fabric and delicately printed accents,
Sandra is a slouchy tapered tote whose billowy body will catch eyes for sure.

SANDRA TOTE

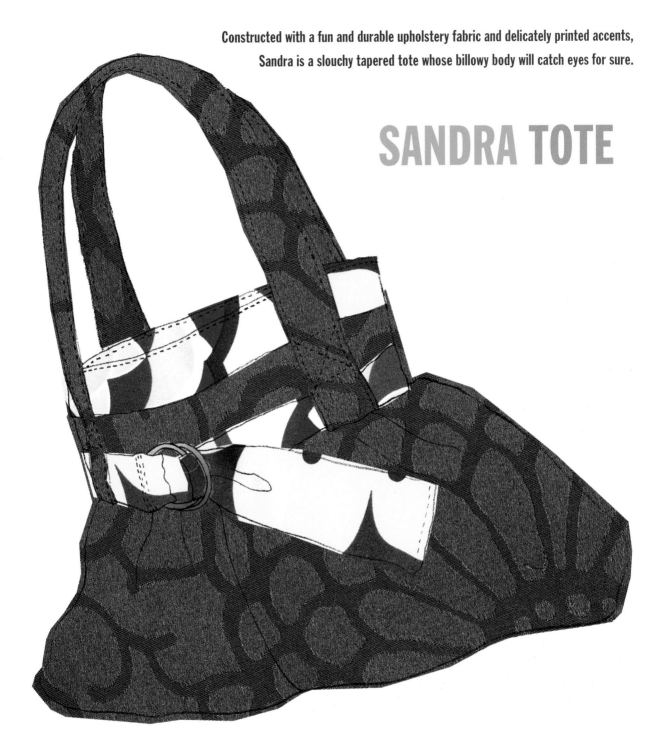

what you need:

½ yd (45.5cm) soft fusible interfacing • ½ yd (45.5cm) heavy fusible interfacing • 1 yd (91cm) heavy upholstery fabric (or any heavy canvas fabric) • ½ yd (45.5cm) cotton print fabric for top detail and belt • Posterboard or large folder for pattern • 1 yd (91cm) soft nonfusible interfacing • ½ yd (45.5cm) matching satin lining fabric • 1 yd (91cm) x ¾" (2cm) elastic • Two 2" (5cm) silver jump rings • Scissors • Sewing machine • Iron and ironing board • Straight pins • Matching color thread • Safety pin

SANDRA **TOTE**

PREP WORK

1. Cut out 2 pieces of heavy fusible interfacing and 2 pieces of upholstery fabric, each measuring 5" (12.5cm) x 30" (76cm). Iron the fusible interfacing to the fabric.

2. Fold and sew two 1½" (3.8cm) wide straps (page 18).

3. Cut 1 piece of cotton print fabric to 36" (91cm) x 5" (12.5cm). This will be used as the belt around the top of the bag.

4. Create a pattern for each piece, based on the dimensions below. You can create the pattern out of posterboard or a large folder.

5. Trace 1 of the main pattern pieces onto soft nonfusible interfacing, and cut it out.

6. Trace 2 of the lining pattern pieces onto soft fusible interfacing, and cut them out.

7. Trace 4 of the top detail pattern pieces onto heavy fusible interfacing, and cut them out.

8. Place the main pattern piece on the wrong side of the upholstery fabric and secure with straight pins along all 4 edges.

Cut it out, using the edge of the pattern piece as a guide for where to cut. Do not remove the straight pins.

9. Place 2 fusible interfacing lining pieces, with the shiny glue side down, on the wrong side of the satin lining fabric. Press with an iron so the entire piece of interfacing fuses to the fabric (page 13).

10. Place 2 of the top detail interfacing pieces, with the shiny glue side down, onto the wrong side of the upholstery fabric. Press with an iron so the entire piece of interfacing fuses to the fabric.

11. Place the other 2 top detail interfacing pieces, with the shiny glue side down, onto the wrong side of the cotton print fabric. Press with an iron so the entire piece of interfacing fuses to the fabric.

12. Cut out all fabric pieces, using the edge of the interfacing as a guide for where to cut.

13. Cut two 14" (35.5cm) pieces of elastic.

skill level: Advanced

pattern dimensions: Main: 28" (71cm) x 20" (51cm) • Lining: 14" (35.5cm) x 14" (35.5cm) • Top Detail: 14" (35.5cm) x 3½" (9cm)

ASSEMBLY

1. Place 1 end of the first strap on top of 1 of the upholstery fabric top detail pieces so that the bottom edge of the strap hangs off 1" (2.5cm) and it's 2" (5cm) in from the left-hand side. Secure with a straight pin.

2. Place the other end of the same strap on top of the same piece of upholstery fabric so the bottom edge of the strap hangs off 1" (2.5cm) and it's 2" (5cm) in from the right-hand side. Secure with a straight pin. Repeat steps 1 and 2 with the other strap and the other top detail upholstery fabric piece.

3. With matching thread, stitch a 1" (2.5cm) box stitch (page 12) on each end of the strap 1½" (3.8cm) above the bottom edge of the top detail upholstery fabric piece (see Diagram 1). Repeat for both top detail pieces of upholstery fabric.

4. For each top detail piece of upholstery fabric, fold the strap down, so it hangs below the bottom of the upholstery fabric piece, and place the right side of the upholstery fabric together with the right side of a cotton print top detail piece. Secure with straight pins.

5. With a ¼" (6mm) seam allowance, sew the top edge of the upholstery fabric top detail piece to the top edge of the cotton detail piece. Do this for both front and back sets of pieces. Open up each piece; they should resemble Diagram 2. Set aside top detail pieces.

6. Turn the main upholstery fabric piece so it's wider than it is tall. Pin the end of the first piece of elastic to the top left-hand corner of the wrong side of the upholstery fabric piece, aligning the length of the elastic with the top of the fabric.

7. Pin the nonfusible interfacing piece to the wrong side of the upholstery fabric. Using ⅛" (3mm) seam allowance, sew 1" (2.5cm) of the elastic to the upholstery fabric and, with your needle still in the fabric, pull the elastic so it stretches to the other end of the top of the main upholstery fabric piece and pin. Sew along the stretched piece of elastic until you reach the other end of the upholstery fabric piece. Repeat steps 6 and 7 with the other piece of elastic on the bottom of the main fabric piece. The elastic will gather the edges of the fabric.

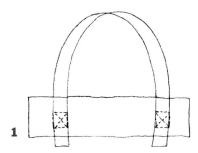

1

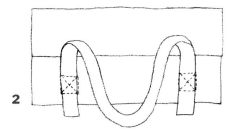

2

SANDRA **TOTE**

8. With right sides together, place one gathered side of the main upholstery fabric piece on a top detail fabric piece (with the strap sewn onto it), aligning the gathered edge of the main piece with the bottom edge of the detail piece. Secure with straight pins. With a ¼" (6mm) seam allowance, stitch the main upholstery fabric piece to the top detail piece.

9. With right sides together, place the other side of the gathered main upholstery fabric piece on the remaining top detail upholstery fabric piece (with the strap sewn to it), aligning the gathered edge of the main piece with the bottom edge of the detail piece. With a ¼" (6mm) seam allowance, stitch the main upholstery fabric piece to the the top detail piece.

10. With right sides together, place the first piece of satin lining fabric on top of the top detail fabric piece so the 14"- (35.5cm-) sides are lined up. With a ¼" (6mm) seam allowance, stitch the top of the lining piece to the top of the detail piece.

11. Repeat the last steps with the opposite lining piece and the other top detail piece. Now all of the detail pieces you cut (aside from the belt piece) should be sewn together in one continuous piece.

12. Fold this piece in half so each gathered edge of the main upholstery fabric piece, the top detail upholstery fabric and cotton pieces, and the lining pieces match up, with right sides together. Secure with straight pins. With a ¼" (6mm) seam allowance, sew along the right- and left-hand sides of this entire piece, leaving the bottoms of the linings open.

13. Turn the entire piece right side out.

14. Create 3" (7.5cm) gussets (page 14) in each bottom corner of the main upholstery fabric piece.

15. Fold the bottom open edge of the lining in 1" (2.5cm) all the way around to get rid of the raw fabric edges and create a nice straight line on the bottom of the bag. Secure with straight pins. With a ¼" (6mm) seam allowance, topstitch all the way across this edge.

16. Stuff the lining and half of the top detail cotton print piece inside the bag, so the lining touches the bottom of the main upholstery fabric piece. Secure the top edge of the bag with straight pins. Topstitch along the top edge of the bag ¼" (6mm) from the top.

17. Fold the piece of fabric for the belt in half lengthwise with right sides together and secure with straight pins.

With a ¼" (6mm) seam allowance, sew down the edge.

18. Attach a safety pin to 1 side of one end of the belt. Insert the attached safety pin into one end of the belt and use the safety pin to guide the belt right side out. Fold each open edge of the belt in 1" (2.5cm) to get rid of the raw fabric edges and create a nice straight line at each end of the belt. Secure with straight pins. Topstitch all the way across both ends of the belt, ¼" (6mm) from the edge.

19. Fold 1 end of the belt over 2" (5cm) and put both silver rings in the fold. Fold the other end of the belt over ½" (13mm) and pin to the other side of the belt. Using ¼" (6mm) seam allowance, stitch back and forth across both fold lines, as shown in Diagram 3.

20. Remove all pins and trim all loose threads.

21. Insert the belt into the belt loops you created when you sewed the straps to the bag. The belt should go around the entire bag and loop through the silver rings in front.

3

what you need:

1 yd (91cm) fusible interfacing • ½ yd (45.5cm) casual cotton print fabric (or use a silk or satin to dress up the bag—something a little dressy, yet sturdy) • Posterboard or large folder for patterns • ½ yd (45.5cm) matching satin lining fabric • 16mm magnetic snap • Scissors • Iron and ironing board • Sewing machine • Straight pins • Matching color thread

A shoulder bag with a flap closure, this handbag can be dressed up or dressed down.

MEREDITH FLAP CLOSURE SHOULDER BAG

PREP WORK

1. Cut out a piece of fusible interfacing and a piece of cotton print fabric to measure 25" (63.5cm) x 5" (12.5cm). These pieces will be used for the strap.

2. Fold and sew one 1½" (3.8cm) wide strap, referring to "Creating Custom Bag Straps from Fabric" (page 18).

3. Create a pattern for both the main piece and the flap piece, based on the dimensions below. You can create the patterns out of posterboard or a large folder.

4. Trace 2 each of the above patterns onto the nonglue side of the fusible interfacing, and cut them out.

5. With the shiny glue side down, place 1 main and 1 flap piece of fusible interfacing onto the wrong side of the cotton fabric. Press with an iron so the entire piece of interfacing fuses to the fabric (page 13).

6. With the shiny glue side down, place the remaining 2 fusible interfacing pieces onto the wrong side of the satin lining fabric. Press with an iron so the entire piece of interfacing fuses to the fabric. Cut out all fabric pieces, using the edge of the interfacing as a guide for where to cut.

ASSEMBLY

1. With right sides together, place the cotton flap piece on top of the cotton main piece so the bottom edge of the flap and the top edge of the main piece are lined up. Make sure the centers of each piece are lined up (see Diagram 1). Secure with straight pins, then sew the pieces together with a ¼" (6mm) seam allowance. Repeat with the 2 corresponding pieces of the lining fabric.

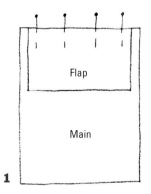

skill level: Intermediate **pattern dimensions:** Main: 14" (35.5cm) x 17" (43cm) • Flap: 12" (30.5cm) x 7" (18cm)

MEREDITH FLAP CLOSURE SHOULDER BAG

2. Open up the piece you stitched in the last step. With right sides together, fold the bottom portion of the main piece up so it lines up with the seam created when the flap was sewn to the main piece. Repeat with the lining piece as well. Secure with straight pins, as shown in Diagram 2.

3. Fold down the top edge of the main piece to create a 1" (2.5cm) lip across the inside on the front of the bag (Diagram 3). Secure with straight pins. Repeat this step with the lining piece.

4. With a ¼" (6mm) seam allowance, straight stitch along both the right- and left-hand sides, as shown in Diagram 4. Repeat this step with the lining piece

5. Create 3" (7.5cm) gussets in the bottom corners of both the cotton fabric and the lining fabric (page 14).

6. With right sides together, place the cotton and lining flaps together so the entire form of the bag is lined up. Secure in place with straight pins at each top corner of the flap and the bottom corners, as well as the folded lip you created.

7. With a ¼" (6mm) seam allowance, stitch both sides and the top of the flap (see Diagram 5).

8. Turn the flap as well as the bottom portion of the cotton fabric right side out. Place the bottom portion of the lining inside the cotton fabric, and line up both of the lips created at the front of the bag with each other.

9. Make a mark in pen an equal distance between each side of the lining fabric, 1" (2.5cm) from the top edge of the flap piece. Insert the outie part of the magnetic snap here (page 19).

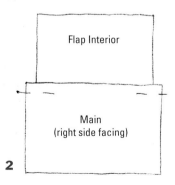

Flap Interior

Main
(right side facing)

2

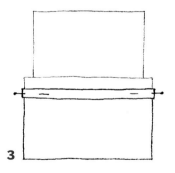

3

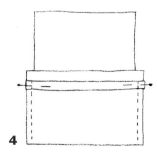

4

10. Fold down the flap with the magnetic snap inserted into it, as if you were closing the bag. Make a mark in pen on the outside fabric piece where the snap falls. Insert the innie part of the magnetic snap at this mark.

11. Turn in all raw edges around the opening of the bag, and line them up with the top edges of the lining. Secure with straight pins.

12. Tuck 1" (2.5cm) of 1 end of the strap in between the layers of the outside fabric and the lining piece, aligning the center of the strap with 1 of the side seams. Repeat with the other end of the strap at the bag's other side seam. Secure with straight pins.

13. Topstitch ¼" (6mm) from the edge, around the entire opening of the bag, including the flap.

14. Remove all pins and trim all loose threads.

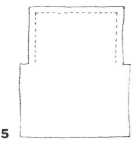

5

RILEY **WRISTLET**

what you need:

Posterboard or large folder for pattern • 1 yd (1m) heavy fusible interfacing • ½ yd (46cm) fabric for outside • ½ yd (46cm) fabric for lining • 14mm Magnetic Snap • Scissors • Iron and Ironing Board • Straight Pins • Sewing Machine • Matching color thread

A fun rounded-style wristlet that can be dressed up or down, depending on what fabric you use to create it.

PREP WORK

1. Create a pattern for the main piece to the dimensions below and according to Diagram 1. Create rounded edges (page 15). You can create the pattern out of poster board or large folder.

2. Trace 2 of the main pattern pieces onto fusible interfacing, and cut out.

3. With the shiny glue side down place 1 of the fusible interfacing pieces on the outside fabric and place the other on the wrong side of the lining piece. Press with an iron so the entire piece of interfacing fuses to the fabric (page 13).

4. Cut out both outside and lining fabric pieces using the edge of interfacing pieces as a guide for where to cut.

5. Pin both pieces together with right sides facing each other, so the shapes line up.

ASSEMBLY

1. Using a ¼" (6mm) seam allowance, sew the outside fabric piece to the lining piece along all edges except the bottom as shown in the diagram below.

2. Turn the clutch right side out, making sure to really round out the rounded edges.

3. Make a pen mark at the top point of the bag piece on the lining side, 1" (2.5cm) down from the top of the point. This is where the outie side of the magnetic snap will be inserted (page 19).

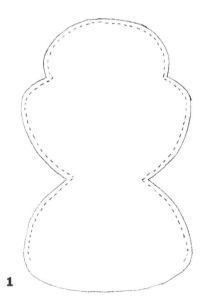

1

skill level: Easy   **pattern dimensions:** Main: 20"T (51cm) x 12"W (30.5cm)

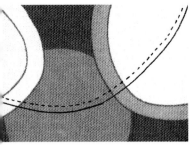

RILEY WRISTLET

4. Fold the bottom open edge of the bag in ¾"(18mm). This will get rid of raw fabric edges and create a clean, straight line on the bottom of the clutch piece. Once the line is straight, use several straight pins to pin this fold in place securely (Diagram 2).

5. Fold the bottom portion of your bag piece so it matches up with the portion above. The 2 pieces should be similar in shape.

6. Fold down the flap and make a pen mark where the outie part of the snap hits the pocket piece of the clutch. This is where the innie part of the magnetic snap will be inserted (page 19).

7. Neatly topstitch along the pinned open edge.

8. Neatly topstitch starting at the bottom right folded edge and continue around the outside of the bag except for the bottom folded edge (Diagram 1).

9. Remove all pins and cut all loose threads.

2

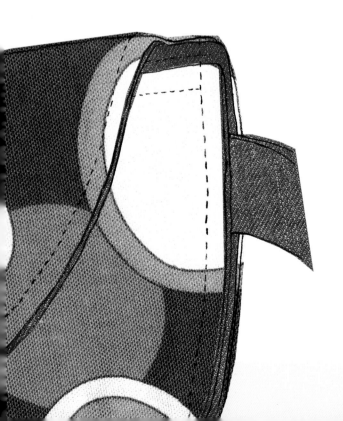

The perfect clutch for an evening out on the town.

DEVON PLEATED CLUTCH

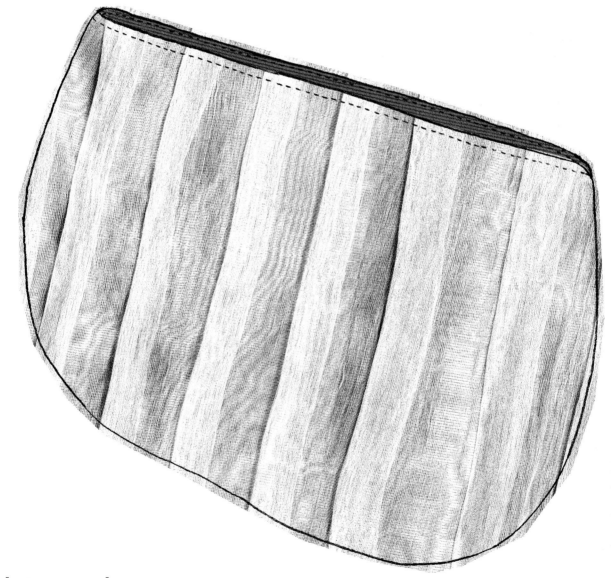

what you need:

Posterboard or large folder for pattern • ½ yd (45.5cm) soft fusible interfacing • ½ yd (45.5cm) satin fabric for exterior • ½ yd (45.5cm) satin lining fabric • 1 yd (91cm) sheer taffeta fabric • Two 14mm magnetic snaps • Sewing machine • Iron and ironing board • Straight pins • Ruler • Pen • Matching thread

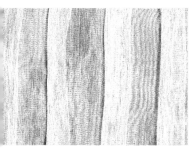

DEVON PLEATED CLUTCH

PREP WORK

1. Create a pattern for the main piece, based on the dimensions. Create rounded edges (page 15). You can create the pattern out of posterboard or a large folder.

2. Trace 4 of the main pattern pieces onto fusible interfacing, and cut them out.

3. With the shiny glue side down, place 2 fusible interfacing pieces, on the wrong side of the satin exterior fabric. Press with an iron so the entire piece of interfacing fuses to the fabric (page 13).

4. With the shiny glue side down, place 2 fusible interfacing pieces, on the wrong side of the satin lining fabric. Press with an iron so the entire piece of interfacing fuses to the fabric.

5. Cut out all fabric pieces, using the edge of the interfacing as a guide for where to cut.

6. Cut two 10" (25.5) x 22" (56cm) pieces of the taffeta fabric.

7. Pin 1 of the taffeta pieces to one of the satin exterior pieces, creating 8 ½" (13mm) gathers vertically. Secure each half inch gather with a straight pin at both the top and the bottom. Repeat with the remaining taffeta and satin exterior pieces.

8. With a ⅛" (3mm) seam allowance, stitch around the entire perimeter of each pinned piece, attaching the taffeta (the sheer overlay) to the satin exterior fabric. This now becomes the bag exterior.

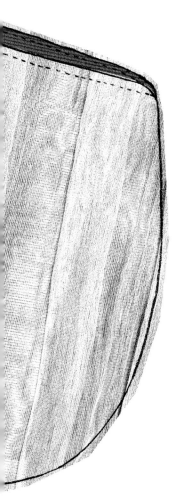

skill level: Intermediate

pattern dimensions: 11" (28cm) wide at the top 16" (40.5cm) wide at the bottom x 12" (30.5cm) high

ASSEMBLY

1. With right sides together, pin 1 bag exterior piece to 1 lining piece, so the shapes line up. Repeat with the remaining bag exterior and lining pieces.

2. With a ¼" (6mm) seam allowance, sew the bag exterior pieces to the lining pieces along the top, straight side.

3. Unfold the pieces just sewn and, with right sides together, place both sewn pieces together, lining up 1 bag exterior piece with the other exterior piece, as well as 1 lining piece with the other piece of lining. Make sure the middle seams line up with each other. Secure with straight pins.

4. Following the stitching lines in the diagram below, stitch these pieces together all the way around, leaving the top section (the lining) open (see Diagram 1).

5. Clip the curved edges, as shown in Diagram 2.

6. Turn the bag right side out, making sure to round out all the edges.

7. With a pen, make 2 marks along the top edge of 1 side of the lining fabric. Marks should be ⅓ and ⅔ of the way across the top and 1" (2.5cm) down from the top edge.

8. Make 2 more marks in pen directly across from the original marks along the top edge of the other side of the lining fabric. Again, marks should be ⅓ and ⅔ of the way across the top and 1" (2.5cm) down from the top edge. Insert the magnetic snaps at these marks (page 19).

9. Fold the bottom open raw edge of the lining in, so it lines up with the edge already sewn. Secure with straight pins. Topstitch along this edge, ¼" (6mm) from the edge, all the way across (page 12).

10. Stuff the lining into the bag.

11. Topstitch all the way around the bag's opening ¼" (6mm) from the top edge.

11. Remove all pins and cut all loose threads.

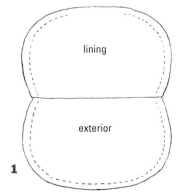

1

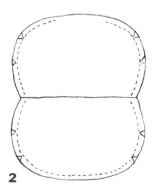

2

what you need:

Posterboard or large folder for pattern   •   1½ yd (1.4m) heavy fusible interfacing   •   ½ yd (45.5cm) heavy cotton fabric (tropical barkcloth looks great)   •   ½ yd (45.5cm) matching satin lining fabric   •   1 yd (91cm) x 1" (2.5cm) grosgrain ribbon   •   One 1" (2.5cm) D ring   •   16mm magnetic snap   •   4 bag feet   •   1 3" (7.5cm) x 10" (25cm) piece of plastic canvas   •   2 circular bamboo handles   • Scissors   •   Sewing machine   •   Iron and ironing board   •   Straight pins   •   Matching thread

Round bamboo handles adorn the top of this tote bag, giving it an exotic flair.

SUZI Q BAMBOO HANDLE TOTE

PREP WORK

1. Create a pattern for the main piece, based on the dimensions below. You can create the pattern out of posterboard or a large folder.

2. Trace 4 of the main pattern pieces onto fusible interfacing, and cut them out.

3. Place 2 fusible interfacing pieces, with the shiny glue side down, on the wrong side of the cotton fabric. Press with an iron so the entire piece of interfacing fuses to the fabric (page 13).

4. Place 2 fusible interfacing pieces, with the shiny glue side down, on the wrong side of the satin lining fabric. Press with an iron so the entire piece of interfacing fuses to the fabric.

5. Cut out all fabric pieces, using the edge of the interfacing as a guide for where to cut.

6. Cut out 2 pieces of cotton fabric measuring 6" (15cm) x 6" (15cm). Fold and sew two 2" (5cm) wide mini-straps, referring to "Creating Custom Bag Straps from Fabric" (page 18). These pieces will be used to attach the bamboo handles.

7. Cut the grosgrain ribbon into one 5" (12.5cm) piece, one 11" (28cm) piece, and one 15" (38cm) piece.

ASSEMBLY

1. Wrap the 5" (12.5cm) piece of ribbon around 1 side of the D ring so the raw edge of the ribbon is in back. Secure with straight pin. Wrap the 11" (28cm) piece of ribbon around the other side of the D ring so the raw edge of the ribbon is in back.

2. Place the ribbon with the D ring onto the right side of one of the cotton fabric pieces, parallel to and 3½" (9cm) down from the top edge. Secure with straight pins (see Diagram 1).

3. Place the entire piece of 15" (38cm) ribbon onto the right side of the other piece of cotton, so the ribbon is 3½" (9cm) down from the top edge. Secure with straight pins.

4. Topstitch along the bottom and top edge of the ribbon on both the front and back pieces of cotton to attach the ribbon belt to both pieces.

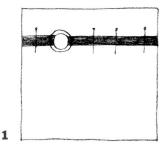

1

skill level: Intermediate   **pattern dimensions:** Main: 14" (35.5cm) x 14" (35.5cm)

SUZI Q BAMBOO HANDLE TOTE

5. With right sides together, pin the cotton pieces together. Make sure the ribbons you sewed in the last step line up. With a ¼" (6mm) seam allowance, sew the cotton pieces together along both sides and the bottom, leaving the top open as shown in Diagram 2.

6. Repeat step 2, using the lining fabric pieces.

7. Create 3" (7.5cm) gussets in the bottom corners of both the cotton fabric and the lining fabric pieces (page 14).

8. Insert a bag foot into each corner of the bottom of the cotton piece (page 15).

9. Turn the cotton piece right side out, and place the lining piece inside the cotton piece.

10. Fold in the top edge of the cotton piece ¾" (2cm). This will eliminate the raw edge. Secure with straight pins.

11. Fold in the top edge of the lining ¾" (2cm), so the top edge aligns with the top edge of the cotton fabric. Secure with the same straight pins used on the cotton.

12. Wrap the mini-straps around the bottom portion of the round bamboo handles. Secure the ends of the straps together with straight pins, as shown in Diagram 3.

13. Tuck the raw edges of the mini-straps in 1" (2.5cm) directly in the middle of the bag between the top of the exterior and lining pieces. Use straight pins to secure them in place.

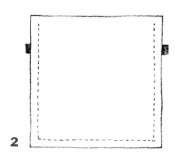

2

3

14. Make a mark in pen on the inside of both the front and back cotton fabric pieces, an equal distance from each side, 1" (2.5cm) from the top edges. Insert the magnetic snap at these marks, referring to "Inserting Magnetic Snaps" (page 19).

15. Topstitch ¼" (6mm) from the top edge of the bag until you return to the point where you started.

16. Remove all pins and cut all loose threads.

specialty bags

ELECTRA ELECTRONIC GADGET BAG

what you need:

½ yd (45.5cm) fusible interfacing • ½ yd (45.5cm) printed cotton fabric • ½ yd (45.5cm) matching satin or cotton lining fabric •
Two zippers at least 2" (5cm) longer than your electronic item • ½ yd (45.5cm) low-loft cotton quilt batting • Ruler • Scissors •
Iron and ironing board • Sewing machine • Straight pins • Matching thread

Create a pattern for a bag to fit and protect just about any electronic item.

PREP WORK

1. Trace the perimeter of the electronic item you intend to store in your new bag onto the nonglue side of the fusible interfacing. Using a ruler, add 3" (7.5cm) around the entire perimeter of the electronic device. This is the pattern. Cut out this pattern and trace it onto the fusible interfacing 3 more times for a total of 4 pieces. Cut out the remaining pieces of interfacing.

2. Trace the pattern onto the printed cotton fabric, and cut it out.

3. With the shiny glue side down, placc 2 of the fusible interfacing pieces onto the wrong side of the uncut printed cotton,

and place the other 2 pieces of interfacing onto the wrong side of the lining fabric. Press with an iron so the entire pieces of interfacing fuse to the fabric. See "Applying Fusible Interfacing" (page 13) for more information.

4. Cut out all fabric pieces, using the edge of the interfacing as a guide for where to cut.

5. Fold over the top of the cotton piece that is not attached to the interfacing 1" (2.5cm), with wrong sides together, and iron to make a crease. This piece will be used for the front pocket.

skill level: Intermediate   **pattern dimensions:** Custom-sized to your electronic gadget

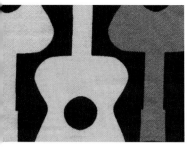

ELECTRA ELECTRONIC GADGET BAG

ASSEMBLY

1. With the right sides together, place the zipper flush with the top of the fold on the pocket piece. Secure with straight pins.

2. Using ⅛" (3mm) seam allowance, sew the top edge of the zipper to the top of the fold on the pocket piece.

3. Place the pocket piece's wrong side against the right side of 1 of the cotton pieces with interfacing. The bottoms should line up and the zipper should fall about ½" (13mm) from the top of the outside fabric piece. Secure with straight pins.

4. With a ⅛" (3mm) seam allowance and right sides together, stitch across the top of the zipper to the cotton fabric.

5. Lay the wrong side of the sewn cotton piece on the quilt batting, and use this as a pattern to cut two pieces of quilt batting the same size as this piece.

6. With the wrong side of the cotton pieces against the quilt batting, pin each sewn and unsewn cotton piece to a piece of the quilt batting of the same size.

7. With right sides together, place the second zipper flush with the top of the cotton piece with the pocket. Secure with straight pins.

8. With a ⅛" (3mm) seam allowance, stitch the top of the zipper to the top of the cotton piece, catching the quilt batting in the seam.

9. With right sides together, place 1 lining fabric piece on top of the remaining piece of cotton (without the pocket). Secure with straight pins.

10. With a ⅛" (3mm) seam allowance, stitch the top of the lining fabric to the top of the cotton.

11. With right sides together, place the other side of the zipper flush with the top of the remaining cotton piece. Secure with straight pins.

12. With a ⅛" (3mm) seam allowance, stitch the top of the zipper to the top of remaining cotton piece.

13. With right sides together, place the remaining lining fabric piece on top of the second cotton piece. Again, the zipper should be in between these two layers. Secure with straight pins.

14. With a ⅛" (3mm) seam allowance, stitch the top of the lining to the top of the cotton.

15. Place the bag so the cotton pieces are lined up with each other and the lining pieces are lined up with each other. The zipper should be in the middle.

16. Open the zipper so the zipper pull is halfway between the right and left side.

17. Secure the open side of the zipper with straight pins.

18. Starting at the lower left-hand corner of the lining, stitch these pieces together all the way around 3 sides, leaving the bottom section of the lining open, as shown in Diagram 1.

19. Open the zipper the rest of the way, so the top is completely open.

20. Turn the bag right side out, making sure to poke out each corner. Chopsticks come in handy for this job. You want them to be squared, rather than rounded. Also, make sure the quilt batting is lying flat.

21. Fold the bottom open edge of the lining in ½" (13mm) on all sides to get rid of the raw fabric edges and create a nice straight line on the bottom of the bag. Once the line is straight, secure with straight pins.

22. Topstitch all the way across this edge ¼" (6mm) from this edge (page 12).

23. Remove all pins and trim all loose threads.

24. Stuff the lining back into the outside of the bag. Make sure the quilt batting lies flat.

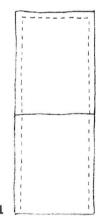

1

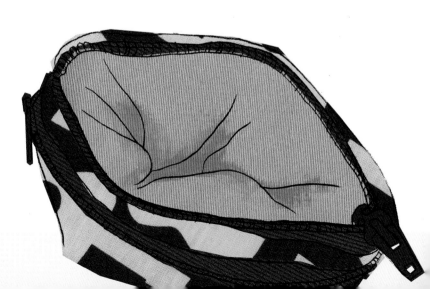

what you need:

Posterboard or large folder for pattern • 2 yd (1.8m) heavy fusible interfacing • 1 yd (91cm) heavy cotton or canvas fabric • 1 yd (91cm) complementary grosgrain satin fabric • Tailor's chalk • 1 yd (91cm) grosgrain ribbon matching the color of the grosgrain satin fabric • Pen • Ruler • Scissors • Sewing machine • Iron and ironing board • Straight pins • Matching thread

Keep all your chargers and electronic accessories safe and in order when you travel.

MAXINE CHARGER BAG

PREP WORK

1. Create a pattern for both the main piece and the flap/pocket piece, based on the dimensions below. You can create the patterns out of posterboard or a large folder.

2. Trace 2 of the main pattern pieces onto fusible interfacing, and cut them out.

3. Trace 2 of the flap/pocket pattern pieces onto fusible interfacing, and cut them out.

4. Trace 1 of the flap/pocket pieces directly onto the cotton or canvas fabric, and cut it out.

5. With the shiny glue side down, place 1 of the main fusible interfacing pieces, onto the wrong side of the cotton or canvas fabric. Press with an iron so the entire piece of interfacing fuses to the fabric (page 13).

6. Place the remaining main fusible interfacing pieces, with the shiny glue side down, on the wrong side of the satin fabric. Press with an iron so the entire piece of interfacing fuses to the fabric.

7. Place 1 of the flap/pocket fusible interfacing pieces, with the shiny glue side down, on the wrong side of the cotton or canvas fabric. Press with an iron so the entire piece of interfacing fuses to the fabric.

8. Place the remaining flap/pocket fusible interfacing pieces, with the shiny glue side down, on the wrong side of the satin fabric. Press with an iron so the entire piece of interfacing fuses to the fabric.

9. Cut out all fabric pieces, using the edge of the interfacing as a guide for where to cut.

ASSEMBLY

1. Fold over the top edge of the cotton or canvas pocket piece that is not attached to the interfacing 1" (2.5cm), wrong sides together, and press with an iron. Fold it over another 1" (2.5cm), press again, and topstitch ¼" (6mm) from edge (page 12).

2. Place the cotton or canvas pocket piece (not attached to the interfacing) on top of the cotton or canvas main piece (attached to the interfacing), so that the bottom edges line up.

skill level: Advanced   **pattern dimensions** Main: 14" (35.5cm) x 30" (76cm) • Flap and Pocket: 10" (25.5cm) x 30" (76cm)

MAXINE CHARGER BAG

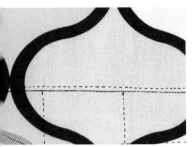

The wrong side of the pocket piece should face the right side of the main outside fabric piece. Secure with straight pins.

3. With a ¼" (6mm) seam allowance, stitch the pocket piece to the cotton or canvas main piece along both sides and the bottom. This will be the main pocket piece.

4. With tailor's chalk, divide the main pocket piece into quarters, making a line at the first quarter, in the middle, and at three quarters across. Stitch along these lines as shown in Diagram 1.

5. With right sides together, place the cotton or canvas flap piece (attached to the interfacing) on top of the satin flap piece (attached to the interfacing). Secure with straight pins.

6. With a ¼" (6mm) seam allowance, stitch along both sides and the bottom. Turn right side out, and topstitch along the same three edges ¼" (6mm) from edge.

7. Place the flap piece on top of the cotton or canvas pocket piece so the top edges line up. The lining side of the flap should be facing the right side of the main pocket piece. Secure with straight pins.

8. With a ¼" (6mm) seam allowance, stitch the top of the flap piece to the pocket piece along the top edge only, as shown in Diagram 2.

9. Fold the piece of grosgrain ribbon in half, and place the fold along the right-hand edge of the bag, so the ribbon is across the main outside fabric piece and the fold sticks out 1" (2.5cm) past the left-hand edge. The ribbon should be halfway between the top and bottom of the outside fabric piece, as shown in Diagram 3. Secure with straight pins.

10. With right sides together, lay the remaining satin fabric piece (attached to the interfacing) on top of the main pocket piece (with the flap now attached). Secure with straight pins in each corner.

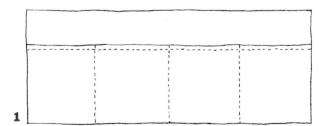

1

2   Exterior Flap

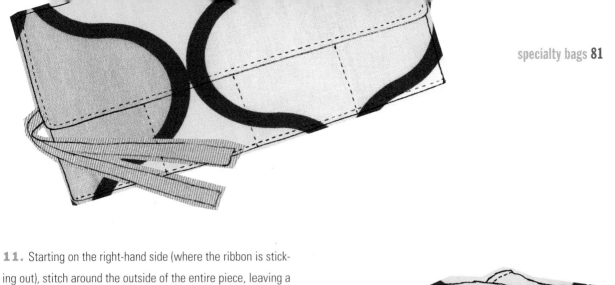

11. Starting on the right-hand side (where the ribbon is sticking out), stitch around the outside of the entire piece, leaving a 6" (15cm) opening on the bottom edge, as shown in Diagram 4.

12. Turn right side out, fold in the remaining raw edge ½" (13mm), and secure with straight pins.

13. Topstitch along the entire bottom edge of the bag.

14. Remove all pins and cut all loose threads.

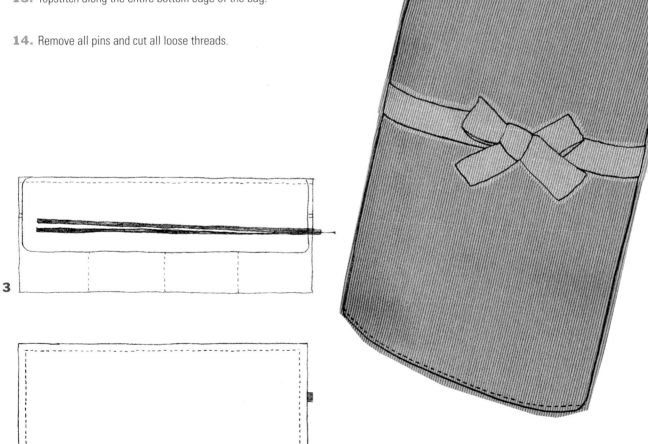

3

4

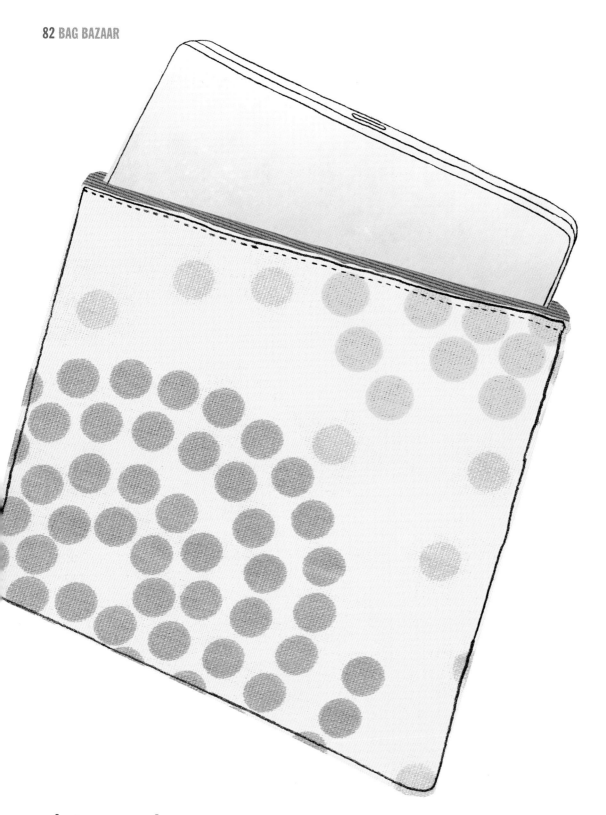

what you need:

1 yd (91cm) soft fusible interfacing   •   ½ yd (45.5cm) cotton or canvas print fabric   •   ½ yd (45.5cm) smooth satin or fleece fabric for lining   •   ½ yd (45.5cm) medium loft cotton quilt batting   •   One 2" (5cm) x 1½" (3.8cm) piece of non-adhesive Velcro   •   Scissors   •   Sewing machine   •   Iron and ironing board   •   Straight pins   •   Ruler   •   Matching thread

This fully padded computer sleeve keeps your laptop clean and protects it from minor bumps and scratches.

ELLEN LAPTOP SLEEVE

PREP WORK

1. Trace the perimeter of your laptop onto the nonglue side of the fusible interfacing. With a ruler add 3" (7.5cm) to the top and bottom edges and 2" (5cm) to the right- and left-hand edges. This is the pattern. Now cut out and trace the pattern onto the fusible interfacing 3 more times.

2. With the shiny glue side down, place 2 of the fusible interfacing pieces onto the wrong side of the cotton or canvas print fabric. Place the other 2 onto the wrong side of the satin or fleece lining fabric. Press with an iron so the entire pieces of interfacing fuse to the fabric (page 13).

3. Cut out all fabric pieces, using the edge of the interfacing as a guide for where to cut.

4. Lay the wrong side of both print fabric pieces on the quilt batting and secure with straight pins in each corner. Using the edge of the fabric as a guide, cut 2 pieces of quilt batting of the same size.

ASSEMBLY

1. Center the hook side of the Velcro piece along the longer edge of 1 of the lining fabric pieces, 1½" (3.8cm) down from the top, and pin in place. The flat, wrong side of the Velcro should be pinned against the right side of the fabric. Repeat this step with the eye side of the Velcro on the remaining piece of lining fabric.

2. Referring to "Box Stitch for Securing Straps" (page 12), boxstitch each side of the Velcro to the pieces of lining fabric they are pinned to, as in Diagram 1. The box should be approximately ⅛" (3mm) smaller than the Velcro piece.

3. Using ¼" (6mm) seam allowance, baste the top (longer) edge of the print fabric to the top edge of the quilt batting. Repeat this step for both print fabric pieces.

4. With right sides together, place 1 piece of the print fabric on top of 1 piece of the lining fabric, so the shapes line up. Pin the remaining print fabric and lining fabric pieces together the same way.

1

skill level: Intermediate   pattern dimensions: Custom-made to fit your laptop

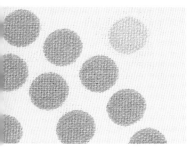

ELLEN LAPTOP SLEEVE

5. With a ¼" (6mm) seam allowance, stitch the print fabric to the lining fabric on the same side you already basted to the quilt batting. Repeat this step for both pieces. Sew with the quilt batting face down and the fabric face up.

6. Unfold the pieces just sewn (leaving the batting against the print fabric) and, with right sides together, line up both pieces. The print fabric of 1 piece should line up with the print fabric of the other, and the lining fabric should line up with the lining fabric. Place pins in each corner as well as at the middle seam. Make sure the middle seams line up with each other.

7. Starting at the lower left-hand corner (the lining), stitch these pieces together all the way around the 2 sides and the top, leaving the bottom section open (see Diagram 2).

8. Turn the sleeve right side out, making sure to poke out the corners. You want them to be squared, rather than rounded. Chopsticks come in handy for this job. Make sure the quilt batting is lying flat.

9. Fold the bottom open edge of the sleeve in ½" (13mm) all the way around to get rid of the raw fabric edges and create a nice straight line on the bottom of the sleeve. Once the line is straight, secure it with straight pins.

10. Using a ¼" (6mm) seam allowance, topstitch (page 12) across this edge.

11. Stuff the lining back into the bag. Make sure the quilt batting is lying flat. The pieces of Velcro on the lining should line up at the top.

12. Topstitch ¼" (6mm) around the top edge of the bag.

13. Remove all pins and trim all loose threads.

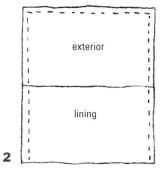

exterior

lining

2

Cut down on the plastic shopping bags, and use this roomy earth-friendly carryall instead.

AURA ECO-FRIENDLY SHOPPING TOTE

what you need:

Posterboard or large folder for pattern • 1½ yd (1.4m) heavy cotton or canvas fabric (the heavier the better) for exterior • 1½ yd (1.4m) lining fabric (the heavier the better) • 2 yd (1.8m) 1–2" (2.5–5cm) heavy-duty nylon webbing for straps • Pen • Scissors • Ruler • Iron and ironing board • Sewing machine • Straight pins • Matching thread

AURA ECO-FRIENDLY SHOPPING TOTE

PREP WORK

1. Create a pattern for the main piece, based on the dimensions below. You can create the pattern out of posterboard.

2. Trace 2 of the main pattern pieces directly onto the exterior fabric, and cut them out.

3. Trace 2 of the main pattern pieces directly onto the lining fabric, and cut them out.

4. Cut 2 30" (76cm) long pieces from the webbing. These 2 pieces will be used for the straps.

ASSEMBLY

1. With right sides together, place the exterior fabric pieces together. Secure with straight pins.

2. With right sides together, place the lining fabric pieces together. Secure with straight pins.

3. With a ¼" (6mm) seam allowance, stitch the exterior fabric pieces together along all edges except the top, as shown in Diagram 1. Repeat this step for the lining fabric pieces.

4. Create 8" (20.5cm) gussets in the bottom corners of both the exterior fabric pieces and the lining fabric pieces (page 14)

5. Turn the exterior fabric and the lining fabric right side out, and place the lining fabric inside the exterior.

1

skill level: Easy **pattern dimensions:** Main: 22" (56cm) x 26" (66cm)

6. Fold down the top edge of the exterior fabric ¾" (2cm). This will eliminate the raw edge. Secure with straight pins.

7. Fold down the top edge of the lining fabric ¾" (2cm) so the top edge aligns with the top edge of the exterior fabric. Secure with same straight pins used on the exterior fabric.

8. Insert 1" (2.5cm) of each raw edge of the first strap into the bag between the exterior and the lining on the front side of the bag. The ends of the this strap should be 3" (7.5cm) from the left- and right-hand side seams. Secure both ends of the strap

with straight pins. Repeat this step for the other strap on the back side of the bag.

9. Topstitch (page 12) around the top of the bag, ¼" (6mm) from the top edge.

10. Topstitch around the top of the bag again, this time 1" (2.5cm) from the top edge.

11. Remove all pins and trim all loose threads.

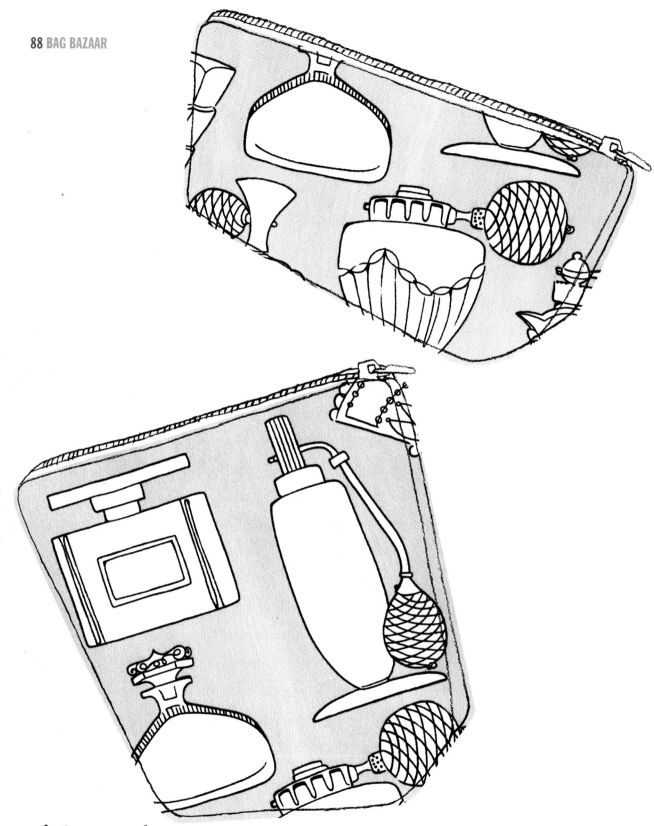

what you need:

Posterboard or large folder for patterns • 1 yd (91cm) fusible interfacing • 1 yd (91cm) oilcloth lining fabric • 1 yd (91cm) printed cotton fabric • Three 12" (30.5cm) zippers • Scissors • Iron and ironing board • Sewing machine • Straight pins • Matching thread

Create the perfect spillproof set of bags for all your cosmetics and toiletries—perfect for storage or travel.

EMILY COSMETIC BAG SET

skill level: Intermediate

pattern dimensions: Emily Small: 11" (28cm) x 6" (15cm) • Emily Medium: 9" (23cm) x 9" (23cm) • Emily Large: 12" (30.5cm) x 12" (30.5cm)

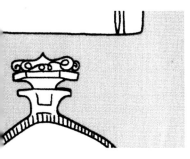

EMILY COSMETIC BAG SET

Note: The following directions can be used for all three sizes of the Emily cosmetic bags.

PREP WORK

1. Create a pattern for all the pieces, based on the dimensions on page 89. You can create the patterns out of posterboard or a large folder.

2. Trace 2 of each pattern piece onto the nonglue side of the fusible interfacing, and cut them out.

3. Trace 2 of each pattern piece onto the oilcloth lining fabric, and cut them out.

4. With the shiny glue side face down, place all 6 fusible interfacing pieces onto the printed cotton fabric. Press with an iron so each piece of interfacing fuses to the fabric (page 13).

5. Cut out all the cotton fabric pieces, using the edge of the interfacing as a guide for where to cut.

ASSEMBLY

1. With right sides together, place a zipper flush with the longer edge of 1 of the cotton fabric. Secure with straight pins.

2. With a ⅛" (3mm) seam allowance, stitch the top of the zipper to the top of the cotton fabric.

3. Place 1 of the oilcloth pieces (of the same size), with right sides together, on top of the cotton fabric piece. The zipper should be in between these two layers. Secure with straight pins.

4. With a ⅛" (3mm) seam allowance, stitch the top of the oilcloth piece to the top of the cotton fabric piece. Open the fabric to expose the zipper.

5. With right sides together, place the other side of the zipper flush with the longer edge of the other cotton fabric piece. Secure with straight pins.

6. With a ⅛" (3mm) seam allowance, stitch the top of the zipper to the top of the other cotton fabric piece.

7. Place the other oilcloth piece, with right sides together, on top of the cotton fabric piece. Again, the zipper should be in between these two layers. Secure with straight pins.

8. With a ⅛" (3mm) seam allowance, stitch the top of the oilcloth piece to the top of the cotton fabric piece.

9. Pin the bag so the cotton and oilcloth pieces are lined up with each other with right sides still together. The zipper should be in between them.

10. Open the zipper so the zipper pull is halfway between the right- and left-hand sides.

11. Secure the open side of the zipper with straight pins.

12. With a ¼" (6mm) seam allowance, starting at the lower left-hand corner (the lining), stitch these pieces together all the way around 3 sides, leaving the bottom section open, as in Diagram 1.

13. Open the zipper the rest of the way, so that the top is completely open.

14. Turn the bag right side out, making sure to poke out the corners. Chopsticks come in handy for this. You want them to be squared, rather than rounded.

15. Create gussets in the bottom corners of the cotton fabric pieces (page 14). The small and medium Emily bags should have 3" (7.5cm) gussets, and the large Emily bag should have 4" (10cm) gussets.

16. Topstitch (page 12) ⅛" (3mm) from the bottom open edge of the lining.

17. Create the same size gussets as in step 15 in the bottom corners of the lining fabric pieces.

18. Remove all pins and trim all loose threads.

19. Stuff the lining into the outside of the bag. Make sure the lining is lying flat inside the bag.

1

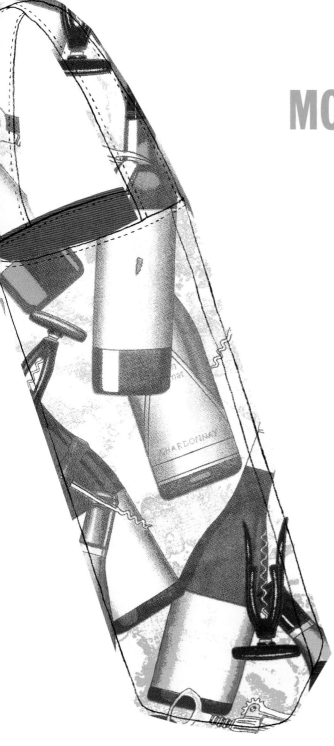

MOONEY WINE TOTE

PREP WORK

1. Cut out 1 piece of fusible interfacing and 1 piece of the barkcloth, each measuring 4" (10cm) x 12" (15cm) for the strap.

2. Fold and sew a 1" (2.5cm) x 12" (30.5cm) strap (page 18).

3. Create a pattern for the main piece, based on the dimensions below. You can create the pattern out of posterboard or a large folder.

4. Trace 2 of the main pattern pieces onto fusible interfacing, and cut them out.

5. With the shiny glue side down, place 1 of the fusible interfacing pieces onto the wrong side of the barkcloth. Press with an iron so the entire piece of interfacing fuses to the fabric (page 13).

6. With the shiny glue side down, place 1 of the fusible interfacing pieces onto the wrong side of the satin lining fabric. Press with an iron so the interfacing fuses to the fabric.

7. Cut out both the barkcloth and satin pieces, using the edge of the interfacing as a guide for where to cut.

what you need:
¾ yd (69cm) heavy fusible interfacing • ½ yd (46cm) vintage barkcloth fabric • Posterboard or large folder for pattern • ½ yd (46cm) matching satin lining fabric • Scissors • Sewing machine • Iron and ironing board • Straight pins • Matching thread

Perfect for toting a special bottle of wine to your favorite BYO restaurant.

ASSEMBLY

1. Fold the barkcloth piece in half lengthwise so the right sides are together. Pin the open side, opposite the fold, together.

2. With a ¼" (6mm) seam allowance, sew together along all edges except the top, as shown in Diagram 1.

3. Repeat the steps 1 and 2, using the satin fabric.

4. Create 3" (7.5cm) gussets in the bottom corners of both the barkcloth and the satin (page 14).

5. Turn the barkcloth piece right side out, and place the satin lining inside.

6. Fold in the top edge of the barkcloth ¾" (2cm). This will eliminate the raw edge. Secure with straight pins.

7. Fold in the top edge of the satin ¾" (2cm), so the top edge aligns with the top edge of the barkcloth. Secure with the same straight pins used on the barkcloth.

8. Tuck 1 side of the strap piece's raw end 1" (2.5cm) between the barkcloth and satin pieces on the left-hand side seam, aligning the center of the strap with the seam. Tuck the other raw end 1" (2.5cm) of the strap between the barkcloth and satin pieces on the right-hand side seam. Use straight pins to secure the strap.

9. Topstitch ¼" (6mm) from the top edge of the bag, all the way around, until you return to the point where you started.

10. Remove all pins and trim all loose threads.

1

skill level: Easy   # pattern dimensions: Main: 14" (35.5cm) x 14" (35.5cm)

what you need:

Posterboard or large folder for pattern • 2 yd (1.8m) heavy fusible interfacing • 1½ yd (1.4m) oilcloth lining fabric • ½ yd (45.5cm) clear plastic fabric (.008–.20 gauge) • 1½ yd (1.4m) heavy cotton fabric • Matching thread • Two 18" (45.5cm) dress zippers • One 10" (25.5cm) x 2" (5cm) piece of elastic • Safety pin • 4 bag feet • Plastic canvas piece measuring 13" (33cm) w x 3" (7.5cm) t • 16mm magnetic snap • 2 yd (2m) x 2" (5cm) nylon webbing • Two 2" (5cm) metal rings • Two 2" (5cm) metal spring hooks • One 2" (5cm) metal slider • 1 yd (91cm) matching grosgrain ribbon • Scissors • Iron and ironing board • Straight pins

Complete with a matching changing pad, this multifunctional baby bag is full of pockets and lined in wipeable, waterproof fabric.

BAILEY BABY BAG

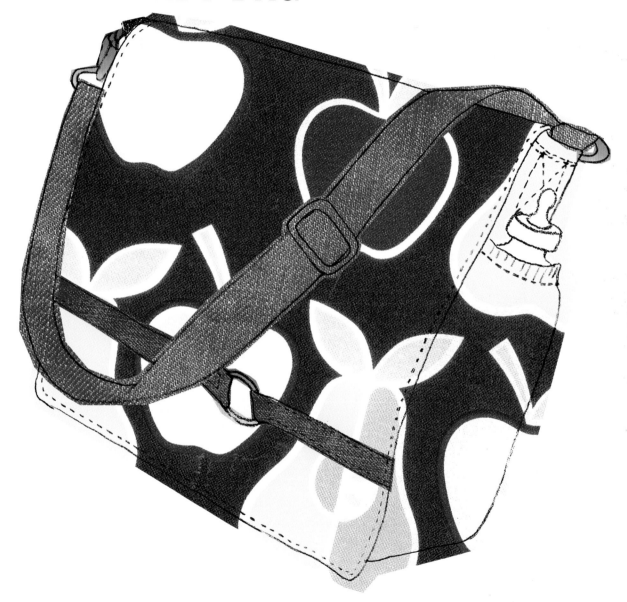

skill level: Advanced

pattern dimensions: Main: 14½" wide (37cm) x 13" (33cm) high • Side: 4" (10cm) wide x 13" (33cm) high • Bottom: 14½" (37cm) x 4" (10cm) • Flap: 14½" (37cm) wide x 16" (40.5cm) high • Pocket: 14½" (37cm) wide x 9" (23cm) high • Changing Mat: 15" (38cm) x 21" (53.5cm)

BAILEY BABY BAG

PREP WORK

1. Create a pattern for all the pieces, based on the dimensions on page 95. You can create the patterns out of posterboard or a large folder.

2. Trace 2 of the main pattern pieces, 2 of the side pattern pieces, 1 of the bottom pattern pieces, 1 of the pocket pattern pieces, 1 of the flap pattern pieces, and 1 of the changing mat pattern pieces onto fusible interfacing, and cut them out.

3. Trace 2 of the side pattern pieces, 1 of the bottom pattern pieces, 3 of the pocket pattern pieces, 1 of the flap pattern pieces, and 1 of the changing mat pattern pieces onto the oilcloth, and cut them out.

4. Trace 1 of the changing mat pattern pieces onto the clear plastic, and cut it out.

5. With the shiny glue side down, place the main, side, bottom, flap, pocket, and changing mat fusible interfacing pieces onto the wrong side of the heavy cotton fabric. Press with an iron so the entire piece of interfacing fuses to the fabric (page 13).

6. Cut out all fabric pieces, using the edge of the interfacing as a guide for where to cut.

7. Cut out two 8" (20cm) x 13" (33cm) pieces of the cotton fabric to use for bottle pockets.

BAG ASSEMBLY

1. With right sides together, pin the main cotton pocket piece to 1 of the oilcloth pocket pieces. With a ¼" (6mm) seam allowance, sew the cotton and oilcloth pocket pieces together along the top, longer edge. Turn right side out.

2. Repeat step 1, this time sewing the remaining 2 oilcloth pocket pieces together.

3. With the right side of zipper on the right side of cotton fabric on pocket, place the edge of 1 of the zippers so it's flush with the top of the first sewn pocket piece and secure it with straight pins, as shown in Diagram 1. With the right side of remaining zipper on the right side of oil cloth fabric, repeat this step with the remaining pocket piece.

4. With a ⅛" (3mm) seam allowance, sew the edge of the zipper to the top edge of the pocket pieces. Repeat for the other pocket pieces.

5. Line up the pocket piece with the cotton fabric and one of the main cotton pieces, so the bottoms (longer sides) are aligned and the zipper faces out. Secure it with straight pins in each bottom corner, as well as along the top zipper, as shown in Diagram 2.

6. With a ¼" seam allowance, stitch along the top edge of the zipper, as well as the bottom edge of the pocket piece, attaching the pocket piece to the main cotton piece.

7. Repeat steps 3 and 4 for the entirely oilcloth pocket piece, attaching it to another of the main oilcloth pieces. Set aside.

8. For each bottle pocket cotton piece, fold 1" (2.5cm) along the shorter top edge, so the wrong sides are together and press. Fold again 3" (7.5cm) and press again. Secure with straight pins.

9. Topstitch ⅛" (3mm) from the bottom fold line (just pinned) of both bottle pocket pieces.

10. Cut the 10" (25.5cm) piece of elastic in half to make two 5" (12.5cm) lengths. Attach the safety pin to 1 of the elastic pieces and insert the pinned end into the tunnel created between the top fold and the seam line of 1 of the bottle pocket pieces in the previous step.

11. Feed the elastic through the tunnel, but before the end of the elastic without the safety pin enters the tunnel, secure this end of the elastic to the edge of the bottle pocket piece with a straight pin. Stitch the end to the edge of the bottle pocket tunnel 3 times to secure it.

12. Fish the end of the elastic with the safety pin attached through the tunnel until it reaches the other end. Since the elastic is shorter than the bottle pocket piece, you will have to stretch the elastic, and when it returns to its natural length, it will gather the pocket fabric. Remove the safety pin and stitch

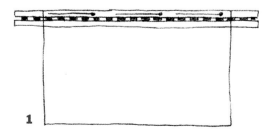

1

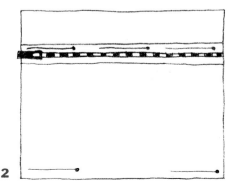

2

BAILEY BABY BAG

the end of the elastic to this end of the bottle pocket tunnel 3 times to secure it.

13. Repeat steps 10–12 for the other piece of elastic and the other bottle pocket.

14. Place the first bottle pocket on top of 1 of the cotton side pieces, aligning the bottoms and gathering the pocket to be 4" (10cm) wide. The right side of the cotton piece should face the wrong side of the bottle pocket. Secure with straight pins.

15. With a ⅛" (3mm) seam allowance, stitch the bottle pocket to the cotton side piece along the 2 sides and the bottom, leaving the top open. Repeat this for both bottle pockets and side pieces.

16. With right sides together, pin both of the side cotton pieces (with bottle pockets attached) to each edge of the outside main fabric

17. With a ¼" (6mm) seam allowance, stitch the side pieces to the main piece.

18. With right sides together, pin the longer edge of the bottom cotton piece to the bottom of the main cotton piece (the one with the pocket attached). With a ¼" (6mm) seam allowance, stitch the bottom piece to the main piece.

19. With right sides together, pin and stitch, with a ¼" (6mm) seam allowance, the other main cotton piece to each of the remaining sides of the outside side pieces.

20. With right sides together, pin and stitch, with a ¼" (6mm) seam allowance, the other main cotton piece to the remaining sides of the bottom cotton piece.

21. With right sides together, stitch the cotton side pieces to the cotton bottom piece. Your entire assembled cotton piece should resemble the shape of a box. Turn it right side out.

22. With a ¼" (6mm) seam allowance, stitch the side pieces to the main piece.

23. With right sides together, pin the longer edge of the bottom oilcloth piece to the bottom of the main oilcloth piece (the one with the oilcloth pocket attached). With a ¼" (6mm) seam allowance, stitch the bottom piece to the main piece.

24. With right sides together, pin and stitch, with a ¼" (6mm) seam allowance, the other main oilcloth piece to each of the remaining sides of the oilcloth side pieces.

25. With right sides together, pin and stitch, with a ¼" (6mm) seam allowance, the other main oilcloth piece to the remaining sides of the bottom oilcloth piece.

26. Stitch the oilcloth side pieces to the oilcloth bottom piece. Your entire assembled oilcloth piece should resemble the shape of a box. Turn it right side out.

27. Insert 1 bag foot (page 15) into each corner of the bottom of cotton piece.

28. Place the oilcloth lining of the bag inside the cotton outside of the bag so the inside pocket is on the front of the bag and the outside pocket is on the back of the bag.

29. Fold in the top edge of the outside cotton portion of the bag ¾" (2cm). This will eliminate the raw edge. Secure with straight pins.

30. Fold down the top edge of the oilcloth lining portion of the bag ¾" (2cm) so the top edge aligns with the top edge of the outside fabric. Secure with the same straight pins used on the cotton fabric.

31. With right sides together, pin the cotton flap piece to the oilcloth flap piece. With a ¼" (6mm) seam allowance, stitch the pieces together along both sides and the bottom.

32. Turn the flap piece right side out.

33. Topstitch (page 12) ¼" (6mm) from the edge around the same 3 sides of the flap you have just sewn,.

34. Make a mark in pen on the oilcloth side of the flap piece an equal distance from each side and 2" (5cm) from the bottom, top-stitched edge. Insert the innie part the magnetic snap (page 19).

35. Tuck 1" (2.5cm) of the raw edge of the flap in between the back cotton and oilcloth main pieces and secure with straight pins as shown in Diagram 3.

36. Fold the flap down, as if you were closing the bag. Make a mark in pen where the first part of the snap hits the main part of the bag. Insert the outie part of the magnetic snap (page 19).

37. Cut two 8" (20cm) pieces of nylon webbing.

38. Wrap each 8" (20cm) length around 1 of the 2" (5cm) rings, and pin the ends of the webbing together (Diagram 4).

39. Stitch halfway between the ring and the raw edge of the webbing wrapped around the ring.

40. Tuck 3" (7.5cm) of the raw end of the webbing (with the ring attached) in between the cotton and oilcloth layers of your bag side pieces, centering the webbing on each side.

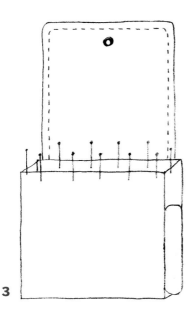

3

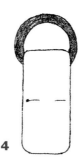

4

BAILEY BABY BAG

41. Topstitch around the top edge of the bag ¼" (6mm) from the top edge, making sure to catch the flap and webbing pieces you pinned in the previous steps, until you return to the point where you started.

42. With thread matching the cotton fabric, stitch a 1½" (3.8cm) box stitch (page 12) on each of the side pieces where the nylon webbing is between the layers of fabric.

43. From the remaining nylon webbing, create an adjustable strap (page 19) that measures 25" (63.5cm) at its shortest length and 50" (127cm) at its longest length.

44. Clip each end of the strap to the rings on the sides of your bag.

CHANGING MAT ASSEMBLY

1. Place the clear plastic changing mat piece on the right side of the cotton changing mat piece. Then place the oilcloth changing mat piece right side down on top of the plastic-covered cotton piece. Secure with straight pins in each corner.

2. Fold the grosgrain ribbon in half and place the fold along the left-hand, shorter edge of the changing mat piece, halfway between the top and the bottom mat piece, so the ribbon lies across the changing mat and the fold sticks out 1" (2.5cm) past the left-hand edge. Secure with straight pins.

3. Starting on the left-hand side (where the ribbon is sticking out), with a ¼" seam allowance, stitch around the outside of the piece, leaving a 6" (15cm) opening on the bottom edge, as shown in Diagram 5. Take care not to catch the ribbon in the seam, except where the fold sticks out of the mat edge.

4. Turn the changing mat right side out, so the clear plastic is on the top, the oilcloth is on the bottom, and 2 ends of the ribbon are on one side. Fold in the remaining raw edge ½" (13mm) and secure with straight pins.

5. Topstitch along all 4 edges of the changing mat.

6. Cut the ends of the grosgrain ribbon at an angle to prevent fraying.

7. Remove all pins and trim all loose threads.

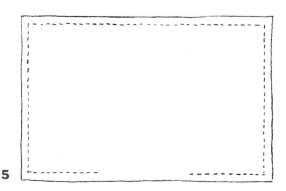

5

Perfect for travel and storage, this simple, lightweight garment bag will protect all your special clothing.

RUBY GARMENT BAG

what you need:

Posterboard or large folder for pattern • 1½ yd (1.4m) heavy upholstery fabric • 36" (91cm) dress zipper
• Scissors • Sewing machine • Clothing hanger • Straight pins • Matching thread

RUBY GARMENT BAG

PREP WORK

1. Create a pattern for the main piece, based on the dimensions below. You can create the pattern out of posterboard or a large folder.

2. Trace 2 of the main pattern pieces onto the wrong side of the fabric, and cut them out.

3. Cut 1 of the fabric pieces in half lengthwise. Each piece will be 10" (25.5cm) x 30" (76cm).

ASSEMBLY

1. Fold the right-hand edge of 1 of the 10" (25.5cm) x 30" (76cm) fabric pieces under ¼" (6mm), with wrong sides together, to eliminate the raw edge. Press with an iron to create a crease. Fold under again ¼" (6mm) and press with an iron to create a crease. Repeat with the left-hand edge of the other piece.

2. With right sides together, place the zipper flush with the folded right-hand edge of the first 10" (25.5cm) x 30" (76cm) piece. Secure with straight pins.

3. With a ⅛" (3mm) seam allowance, stitch the zipper to the edge of the fabric.

4. With right sides together, place the other side of the zipper on the folded left-hand edge of the other 10" (25.5cm) x 30" (76cm) piece of fabric. Make sure both pieces of fabric are aligned. Secure with straight pins.

skill level: Intermediate   **pattern dimensions:** 20" (51cm) x 30" (76cm)

5. With a ⅛" (3mm) seam allowance, stitch the zipper to the edge of the fabric.

6. Open the fabric sewn to the zipper so the zipper falls directly in the middle. With right sides together, place this piece of fabric against the 20" (51cm) x 30" (76cm) fabric piece, making sure the zipper falls in the middle of the main fabric piece without the zipper. Trim the extra fabric on the right- and left-hand edges of the fabric piece without the zipper, so both fabric pieces are the same size.

7. With a ¼" (6mm) seam allowance, stitch the 2 outside fabric pieces together along all edges except for 6" (15cm) along the top, as shown in Diagram 1. Use caution when you sew over each end of the zipper.

8. Turn the bag right side out.

9. Fold in the top raw edge of the bag piece ¼" (6mm) and iron it to make a crease line. Fold this edge again ¼" (6mm) and iron it to make a crease line. Secure with straight pins.

10. Topstitch (page 12) across the all the way top opening of the bag, ¼" (6mm) from the top folded edge. Again, use caution when sewing across the zipper.

11. Remove all pins and trim all loose threads.

1

what you need:

Posterboard or large folder for the pattern • 3½ yd (3.2m) heavy fusible interfacing • 1 yd (91cm) waterproof lining fabric (oilcloth works great) • 2 yd (1.8m) x 1–2" (2.5–5cm) of any color nylon webbing for straps • 1 yd (91cm) heavy weight cotton or canvas fabric (any color, any texture) for exterior • 16mm magnetic snap • Scissors • Sewing machine • Iron and ironing board • Straight pins • Matching thread

This roomy tote has a waterproof interior for easy cleanup when you return from the beach.

SHIRLEY BEACH TOTE

PREP WORK

1. Create a pattern for the main piece and the pocket, based on the dimensions below. You can create the pattern out of posterboard or a large folder.

2. Trace 2 of the main pattern pieces onto the fusible interfacing, and cut them out.

3. Trace 2 of the main pattern pieces directly onto the wrong side of the waterproof lining fabric, and cut them out.

4. Trace 2 of the pocket pattern pieces directly onto the wrong side of the lining fabric, and cut them out.

5. Cut two 30" (76cm) long pieces from the nylon webbing. These 2 pieces will be used for the straps. **Note:** If you would like to have the straps made from the same fabric you are using for your bag (page 18), cut out two 30" (76cm) long x 4" (10cm) wide pieces of fabric and use this fabric to cover the nylon webbing pieces.

6. With the shiny glue side down, place both fusible interfacing pieces onto the wrong side of the exterior fabric. Press with an iron so the entire pieces of interfacing fuse to the fabric (page 13).

7. Cut out both exterior fabric pieces, using the edge of the interfacing as a guide for where to cut.

ASSEMBLY

1. With right sides together, pin the exterior fabric pieces together.

2. With a ¼" (6mm) seam allowance, stitch the 2 exterior fabric pieces together along all edges except the top (the longer side), as shown in Diagram 1.

3. Repeat steps 1 and 2 for the 2 pocket pieces.

4. Turn the pocket piece right side out, making sure to poke out the corners. You can use a chopstick to do this. You want them to be squared off, rather than rounded.

5. Fold the open edge of the pocket piece in 1" (2.5cm) to get rid of the raw edge of the fabric. Once the edge is straight, secure with straight pins, as shown in Diagram 2 on page 106.

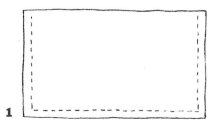

skill level: Intermediate

pattern dimensions: Main: 22" (56cm) x 16½" (42cm) • Pocket: 18" (45.5cm) x 16½" (42cm)

SHIRLEY BEACH TOTE

6. Fold the pocket piece in half crosswise, and create a crease line to mark the middle of this rectangular pocket. Mark the ends of the crease line with straight pins.

7. Fold 1 of the main lining fabric pieces in half the same way you did for the pocket and make a crease line down the middle. Mark the ends of the crease line with straight pins.

8. Place the pocket piece on the crease of the main lining fabric piece, so the middle straight pin markers line up (both pieces should be right side up). The bottom edge of the pocket should be 3" (7.5cm) from the bottom edge of the main lining fabric piece. Attach the pocket to the main lining fabric piece with straight pins in each corner.

9. Starting 2" (5cm) below the top right-hand corner of the pocket, sew up 2" (5cm) to the right-hand corner. Continue sewing about ½" (13mm) across the top and back to the side seam, making a small triangle in the corner (see Diagram 3). Continue sewing along the side pocket seam all the way to the bottom right-hand corner. Continue sewing halfway across

the bottom until you get to the middle crease line. Allow the stitch to follow the middle crease line to the top of the pocket. When you reach the top of the pocket, pivot the fabric (with the needle still in the fabric) and follow the stitch line back down to the bottom seam. Continue this seam to the left-hand corner and up the left-hand side seam of the pocket. Make another small triangle at the top left-hand corner, as you made at the top right-hand corner, and end the stitching 2" (5cm) from the top of the left-hand side.

10. With right sides together, pin both lining fabric pieces together. (One now has the pocket piece sewn to it.) With a ¼" (6mm) seam allowance, sew the 2 lining fabric pieces together along three edges, leaving the top open as you did with the exterior fabric pieces in step 2.

11. Create 4" (10cm) gussets (page 14) in the bottom corners of both the exterior fabric and lining fabric pieces.)

12. Turn the exterior fabric piece right side out.

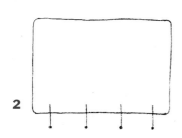

2

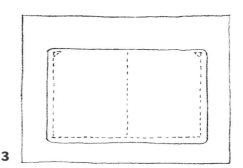

3

13. Make a mark in pen on the inside of the lining fabric piece, an equal distance from each side and 1½" (3.8cm) from the top edge on both the front and back. Insert the magnetic snap (page 19) here.

14. Pin 1 end of the first nylon webbing strap piece to the right side of the bag exterior piece, 4" (10cm) from 1 side of the bag, and the other end of the same nylon webbing piece 4" (10cm) from the other side of your bag. Be sure to leave at least 1" (2.5cm) of the strap sticking out above the top edge of the bag. Repeat the same step with the second nylon webbing strap piece on the other side of the bag. See Diagram 4.

15. Place the exterior fabric piece inside the lining fabric piece so that the right sides are facing each other and the straps are hanging in between the two layers. Pin the two layers together along the top edge.

16. Using ¼" (6mm) seam allowance, sew the exterior fabric piece to the lining fabric piece along the top edge. When you are sewing across where the nylon strap pieces are sticking out, be sure to stitch back and forth a few times to ensure a stronger stitch. Continue sewing around the top edge, but leave about a 6" (15cm) unsewn gap between the front straps to turn the bag.

17. Reach into the 6" (15cm) gap at the top, turn the exterior fabric piece right side out, and push the lining fabric into the bag exterior.

18. Fold in the raw edges of fabric that are sticking out of the gap left open in step 16, and pin them so they are level with the top of the rest of the bag.

19. Topstitch this gap closed along the top edge, ¼" (6mm) from the top edge.

20. Remove all pins and trim all loose threads.

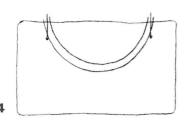

4

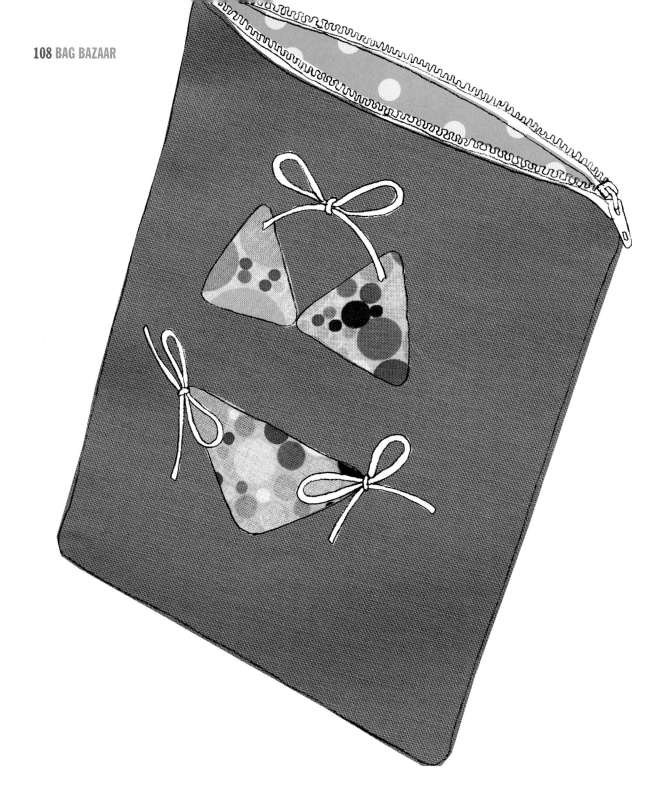

what you need:

Posterboard or large folder for patterns • ½ yd (45.5cm) fusible interfacing • ½ yd (45.5cm) oilcloth lining fabric • ½ yd (45.5cm) solid-color cotton fabric for exterior • ¼ yd (23cm) Pellon Wonder Under • ¼ yd (23cm) print fabric • One 12" (30.5cm) zipper • 1 yd (91cm) satin rat-tail cord • Scissors • Hand-sewing needle • Iron and ironing board • Sewing machine • Straight pins • Matching thread

Keep your other packed clothes dry with the cutest little waterproof storage bag for your wet bikini.

AMANDA WET BIKINI BAG

PREP WORK

1. Create a pattern for the main piece, based on the dimensions below. You can create the pattern out of posterboard or a large folder.

2. Create patterns for the bikini cutout, using larger scaled version of the shapes in Diagram 1 as guides.

3. Trace 2 pieces of the bag pattern from Step 1 onto the wrong side of the oilcloth lining fabric.

4. Trace 2 pieces of the bag pattern onto the nonglue side of the fusible interfacing and cut them out.

5. With the shiny glue side down, place the fusible interfacing pieces onto the wrong side of the solid cotton fabric. Press with an iron so the entire pieces of interfacing fuse to the fabric (page 13).

6. Cut out the solid fabric pieces, using the edge of the interfacing as a guide for where to cut.

7. Trace the bikini cutout pattern (Diagram 1) onto the paper side of the Wonder Under, spacing the pieces at least 4" (10cm) away from each other. Cut out the shapes, adding at least 2" (5cm) around the actual shape of each piece.

8. Place the shiny side of the Wonder Under (page 13) pieces directly onto the wrong side of the print fabric and iron following the manufacturer's instructions.

9. Using the traced shapes of the bikini pieces as your guides, cut out both the layer of Wonder Under and the layer of print fabric.

1

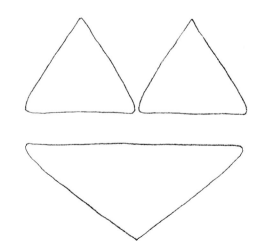

skill level: Intermediate   **pattern dimensions:** 11" (28cm) x 9" (23cm)

AMANDA WET BIKINI BAG

10. Peel away the paper backing and place the shiny side of the Wonder Under pieces directly on the front of 1 of the solid exterior fabric pieces, using Diagram 2 as a guide for placement. Carefully iron all three bikini pieces onto 1 of the solid exterior fabric pieces.

ASSEMBLY

1. With right sides together, place the zipper flush with the top, shorter edge of the exterior fabric piece with the bikini cutouts, which will be the front of the bag. Secure with straight pins.

2. With a ⅛" (3mm) seam allowance, sew the top of the zipper to the top of the exterior fabric.

3. With right sides together, place 1 of the oilcloth pieces (of the same size) on top of the exterior fabric piece. The zipper should be in between these two layers. Secure with straight pins.

4. With a ⅛" seam allowance, stitch the top edge of the oilcloth to the top edge of the exterior fabric.

5. With right sides together, place the other side of the zipper flush with the top edge of the other exterior fabric piece. Secure with straight pins.

6. With a ⅛" (3mm) seam allowance, stitch the top of the zipper to the top of this exterior fabric piece.

7. With right sides together, place the remaining oilcloth piece on top of the second exterior fabric piece. Again, the zipper should be in between these two layers. Secure with straight pins.

8. With a ⅛" (3mm) seam allowance, stitch the top edge of the oilcloth piece to the top edge of the exterior fabric piece.

9. Pin the bag so the exterior fabric pieces are lined up with each other and the oilcloth pieces are lined up with each other. The zipper should be in between them.

10. Open the zipper so the zipper pull is halfway between the right- and the left-hand sides.

11. Secure the open side of the zipper with straight pins.

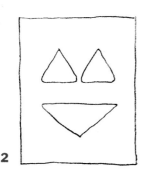

2

12. Starting at the lower left-hand corner (the lining), stitch these pieces together all the way around three sides, leaving the bottom section open, as in Diagram 3.

13. Open the zipper the rest of the way, so that the top is completely open.

14. Turn the bag right side out, making sure to poke out your corners. Chopsticks come in handy for this job. You want them to be squared, rather than looking rounded.

15. Fold the bottom open edge of the lining in 1" (2.5cm) all the way around to get rid of the raw fabric edges and create a nice straight line on the bottom of your bag. Once the fabric is straight, pin this fold into place securely with several straight pins.

16. Topstitch (page 12) along this edge all the way across.

17. Remove all pins and trim all loose threads.

18. Stuff the lining back into the bag exterior. Make sure the lining lies flat inside the bag.

19. Cut the satin rat-tail cord into three 12" (30.5 cm) pieces. Tie all three pieces into little bows.

20. With matching color thread, hand-sew these decorative bows to the front exterior fabric at the points on the bikini shown in Diagram 4.

Top

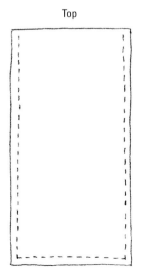

3

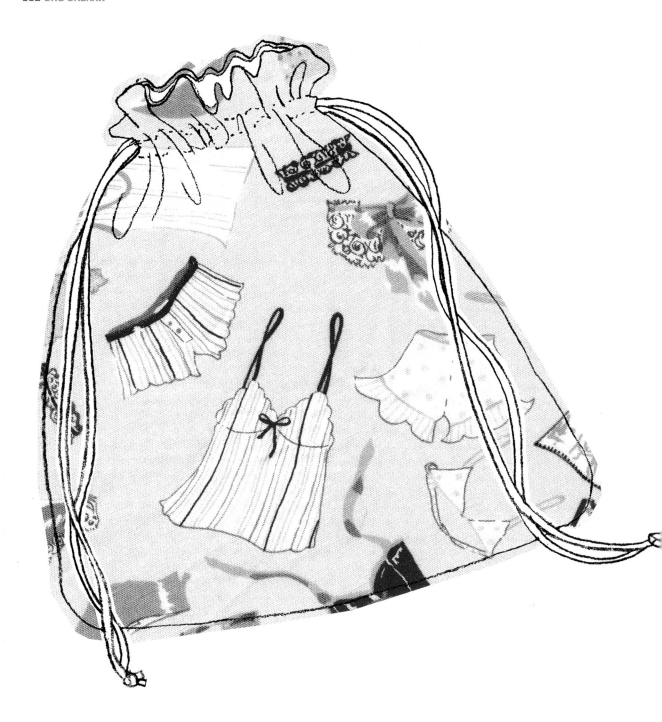

what you need:

Posterboard or large folder for pattern • ¼ yd (23cm) silk or satin fabric for exterior • ¼ yd (23cm) silk or satin lining fabric •
2 yd (1.8m) satin rattail cord • Safety pin • Tailor's chalk • Scissors • Sewing machine • Iron and ironing board • Straight
pins • Matching thread

Keep your unmentionables organized while traveling with this sweet drawstring lingerie bag.

CELESTE LINGERIE BAG

PREP WORK

1. Create a pattern for the main piece, based on the dimensions below. You can create the pattern out of posterboard or a large folder.

2. Carefully, trace 2 of the pattern pieces directly onto the wrong side of the silk or satin exterior fabric and cut them out. Silky fabric will tend to slip and slide around while tracing, so use caution.

3. Trace 2 of the pattern pieces directly onto the wrong side of the silk or satin lining fabric and cut them out.

4. Fold the satin rattail cord in half and place a safety pin at the point halfway between the 2 ends.

ASSEMBLY

1. With right sides together, pin 1 of the exterior fabric pieces to 1 of the lining fabric pieces. Repeat this step with the remaining exterior and lining fabric pieces.

2. Stitch the top (1 of the shorter sides) of the fabric piece to the top of the lining fabric piece.

3. Repeat step 2 with the remaining exterior and lining fabric pieces.

4. Open up each piece you just stitched so the right sides of the exterior and lining fabric on both pieces face you.

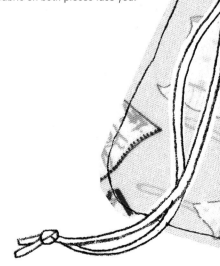

skill level: Intermediate   **pattern dimensions:** Main: 14" (35.5cm) x 13" (33cm)

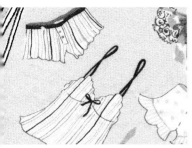

CELESTE LINGERIE BAG

5. With right sides together, pin both of these pieces together, so the exterior fabric pieces line up with each other and the lining fabric pieces line up with each other. The stitch lines from steps 2 and 3 should also line up. See Diagram 1.

6. Using tailor's chalk, make two star marks 1" (2.5cm) from both the left- and right-hand edges, ½" (13mm) from the middle seam and 1" (2.5cm) from each other vertically, on the exterior fabric piece (see Diagram 1).

7. Stitch the 2 pieces together, starting at 1 of the long sides, and continuing around the short side of the exterior fabric and back around down the long side, leaving the space between the star marks on each side unstitched. The short side of the lining fabric should also remain unstitched. See Diagram 2.

8. Turn the entire piece right side out.

9. Fold the raw edge of the lining fabric in 1" (2.5cm) and secure with straight pins. Topstitch (page 12) along ¼" (6mm) from the bottom folded edge.

10. Stuff the lining portion of the bag inside the exterior fabric piece, making sure the stitched seam between the exterior fabric and the lining is even.

11. With tailor's chalk, draw a line around the exterior fabric at the point where the hole in each side seam begins. Draw another line around the top of the exterior fabric, below the line you just drew, where the hole in each side seam ends.

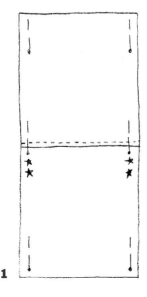

1

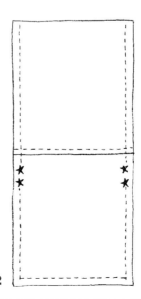

2

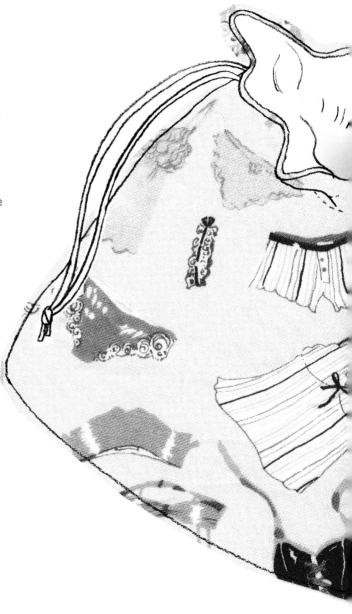

12. Topstitch along both of these lines. See Diagram 3.

13. To thread the rattail cord, insert the safety pin end into one of the side seam holes. Push the safety pin, attached to the cord, in between the layers of fabric until it reaches the hole on the opposite side seam.

14. Detach the safety pin and cut the cord at the fold, so there are now two pieces of cord. By pulling 1 end of 1 of the cords, determine which is the other end of this cord. Tie the ends of the same cord together in a neat knot. Tie the ends of the other cord together in another neat knot.

15. Trim all loose threads.

3

Use this handy cylindrical bag to carry your yoga mat to and from class.

KENDRA YOGA MAT TOTE

PREP WORK

1. Create a pattern for both the main piece and the flap piece, following the dimensions below. You can create the patterns out of posterboard or a large folder.

2. Trace 4 of the main pattern pieces onto fusible interfacing, and cut them out.

3. Trace 2 of the flap pattern pieces onto fusible interfacing, and cut them out.

4. With the shiny glue side down, place 2 of the main fusible interfacing pieces onto the wrong side of the cotton fabric. Press with an iron so the entire pieces of interfacing fuse to the fabric (page 13).

5. With the shiny glue side down, place the 2 remaining main interfacing pieces onto the wrong side of the nylon lining fabric. Press with an iron so the entire pieces of interfacing fuse to the fabric.

6. With the shiny glue side down, place 1 of the flap fusible interfacing pieces onto the wrong side of the cotton fabric. Press with an iron so the entire piece of interfacing fuses to the fabric.

7. With the shiny glue side down, place the remaining flap fusible interfacing piece onto the wrong side of the nylon fabric. Press with an iron so the entire piece of interfacing fuses to the fabric.

8. Cut out all fabric pieces, using the edge of the interfacing as a guide for where to cut.

what you need:

Posterboard or large folder for tracing pattern • 2 yd (1.8m) heavy fusible interfacing • 1 yd (91cm) breathable cotton fabric • 1 yd (91cm) breathable nylon lining fabric (B) • 1½ yd (1.4m) x 2" (5cm) nylon webbing • 16mm magnetic snap • Scissors • Sewing machine • Iron and ironing board • Straight pins • Matching thread

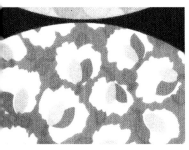

KENDRA YOGA MAT TOTE

ASSEMBLY

1. With right sides together, pin the 2 main lining fabric pieces together. With a ¼" (6mm) seam allowance, sew the lining pieces together along all edges except the top. See Diagram 1.

2. Repeat the previous step with the 2 cotton fabric pieces, but this time place 1 end of the nylon webbing strap piece in between the fabric layers on the bottom, the shorter side. Center the strap between the edges of the cotton fabric and allow the strap to stick out 1" (2.5cm) below the bottom of the bag. When sewing the bottom seam, sew back and forth a few times over the strap to ensure a strong stitch. Be careful not to catch the long end of the strap in the side seams.

3. Create 3" (7.5cm) gussets (page 14) in the bottom corners of both the cotton fabric pieces and lining fabric pieces.

4. Turn the cotton fabric piece right side out, and place the lining fabric piece inside.

5. Fold in the top edge of the cotton fabric ¾" (2cm). This will eliminate the raw edge. Secure with straight pins.

6. Fold in the top edge of the lining fabric ¾" (2cm) so it aligns with the top edge of the cotton fabric. Secure with the same straight pins used on the cotton.

7. With right sides together, pin the cotton flap piece to the lining fabric flap piece. With a ¼" (6mm) seam allowance, stitch the 2 fabric pieces together along both long sides and the bottom, shorter side.

8. Turn the flap piece right side out.

1

skill level: Intermediate

pattern dimensions: Main piece: 28" (71cm) high x 10" (25.5cm) wide • Flap: 10" (25.5cm) high x 8" (20.5cm) wide

9. Topstitch (page 12) ¼" (6mm) from the edge around the same 3 sides of the flap you have just sewn.

10. Make a mark in pen on the lining side of the flap piece, an equal distance between each side and 2" (5cm) from the bottom, topstitched edge. Insert the outie part of the magnetic snap (page 19).

11. Tuck 1" (2.5cm) of the raw edge of the flap in between the cotton fabric and the lining fabric on the main bag pieces, and secure with straight pins, as shown in Diagram 2.

12. Fold the flap down, as if closing the bag. Make a mark in pen where the outie part of the snap hits the main part of the bag. Insert the innie part of the magnetic snap.

13. Tuck at least 1" (2.5cm) of the loose end of the nylon webbing strap in between the flap and the main cotton fabric piece, an equal distance from each side seam. Secure with a straight pin.

14. Topstitch around the top edge, ¼" from the top of the bag, making sure to catch the flap and the webbing strap, until you return to the point where you started.

15. Remove all pins and trim all loose threads.

2

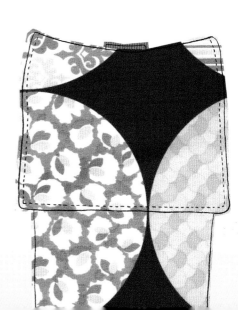

TAMARA BELT BAG

what you need:

Poster Board or large folder for patterns • ¼ yd (.25m) outside (canvas) fabric • ¼ yd (.25m) lining fabric • ¼ yd (.25m) fusible interfacing • 1 12" (18cm) zipper • Scissors • Iron and ironing board • Sewing machine • Straight pins • Matching thread • Safety pin

This hip alternative to the "fanny pack" easily slides onto your favorite belt leaving your hands free.

PREP WORK

1. Create a pattern for the pattern piece using the dimensions below. You can create the patterns out of poster board or a large folder.

2. Trace 4 each of above pattern onto the non-glue side of the fusible interfacing, and cut them out.

3. Place 2 pieces of the fusible interfacing pieces onto the outside fabric. Be sure to place interfacing with shiny glue side down, onto the wrong side of outside fabric. Press with iron so the entire piece of interfacing fuses to the fabric (page 13).

4. Place 2 pieces of the fusible interfacing pieces onto the fabric you will be using the lining fabric. Be sure to place interfacing with shiny glue side down, onto the wrong side of outside fabric. Press with iron so the entire piece of interfacing fuses to the fabric.

5. Cut out all 4 fabric pieces using the edge of the interfacing pieces as a guide for where to cut.

6. Cut out 2 pieces of outside fabric to measure 6" (15cm) x 3" (7.5cm). These will make the belt loops.

ASSEMBLY

1. With right sides together, fold the 2 small pieces of outside fabric in half lengthwise. Sew across the raw edges of the open sides of fabric on each piece, creating a tube.

2. Using a safety pin, turn each tube right side out and iron flat.

3. Place each of the flattened tubular pieces (the belt loops) onto 1 of the outside pieces so it extends from top to bottom as shown in the illustration on page 123. Each belt loop should be placed 2" (5cm) from each side. Each piece should extend past your outside piece by ½" (13mm) on the top and bottom. Secure with straight pins.

skill level: Intermediate   **pattern dimensions:**   11"w (28cm) x 5"t (12.5cm)

TAMARA BELT BAG

4. Stitch the top and bottom of each belt loop to the piece of outside fabric it's pinned to.

5. With right sides together, place the zipper flush with the top of the outside fabric piece with the belt loops attached to it. Secure with straight pins.

6. Sew the top of the zipper to the top of the outside fabric piece.

7. Place 1 of the lining fabric pieces (of the same size), with right sides together, on top of the outside fabric piece. The zipper should be in between these two layers. Secure with straight pins

8. Sew the top of the lining to the top of the outside fabric piece.

9. With right sides together, place the other side of the zipper flush with the top of the other outside fabric piece. Secure with straight pins.

10. Sew the top of the zipper to the top of the other outside fabric piece.

11. Place the other lining fabric piece, with right sides together, on top of the outside fabric piece. The zipper should again, be in between these two layers. Secure with straight pins.

12. Sew the top of the lining to the top of the outside fabric piece.

13. Pin the bag so the outside fabric pieces are lined up with each other and the linings are lined up with each other. The zipper should be in between those pieces.

14. Open the zipper so the zipper pull is half way between the right and left side.

15. Secure the open side of the zipper with straight pins.

16. Starting at the lower left hand corner, stitch these pieces together all the way around three sides, leaving the bottom section open.

17. Open the zipper the rest of the way, so the top is completely open.

18. Turn the bag right side out, making sure to poke out the corners of the bag. You want them to be squared, rather than rounded.

19. Fold the bottom open edge of the lining in 1" (2.5cm) all the way around to get rid of the raw fabric edges and cre-

ate a straight line on the bottom of your bag. Once the line is straight, use several straight pins to pin this fold into place securely.

20. Topstitch all the way across this edge.

21. Remove all pins and cut all loose threads.

22. Stuff the lining back into the outside of the bag. Make sure the lining is lying flat inside the bag.

Templates

Kate Hobo Bag (page 48)

Enlarge 313%

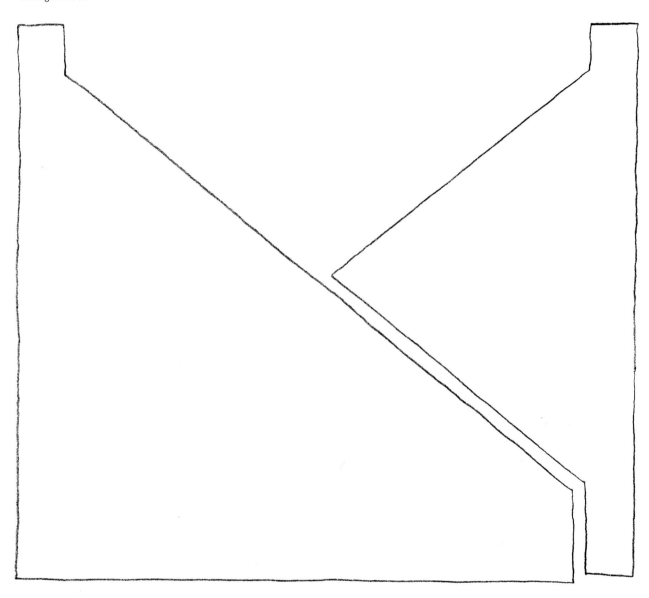

Creating your Own Patterns for Bags

It's easy to create basic-shaped bags in just about any size you want. Just use this easy formula and ¼" (6mm) seam allowances to back into whatever sized bag you are creating.

Pattern Width = Finished Depth + Finished Width + ½" (13mm)

Pattern Height = ½ Finished Depth + Finished Height + 1½"(3.8cm)

So for example if you would like to create a rectangle shaped tote that is 12" (30.5cm) tall x 15" (38cm) wide and 3" (7.5cm) deep, use the following formula to figure out the pattern size.

Pattern Width = 3 (7.5cm) + 15″ (38cm) + ½" (13mm)
Pattern Width = 18.5"W

Pattern Height = 1½" (3.8cm) + 12" (30.5cm) + 1½" (3.8cm)
Pattern Height = 15"T

Refer to our Suzi Q Pattern (page 68) for more explicit directions on applying this formula to create whatever size bag you'd like.

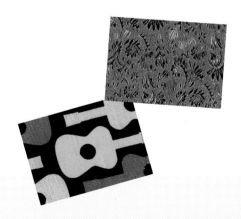

Glossary

appliqué a cutout decoration attached to a larger piece of material by sewing or adhesive

backstitch a stitch taken backwards to reinforce the beginning and end of each seam

baste a method of temporarily joining fabric, using large stitches, which are easily removed

clean finish a row of stitches ¼" (6mm) from the edge, pressed to the wrong side; if the raw edge will not be stitched down in another step, stitch them down

grosgrain a type of tightly woven ribbon or fabric with a ribbed texture

lining a lighter-weight fabric used for the inside of a bag; it can be the same color as the outside of the bag, or a different color for more visual interest

innie the side of the magnetic snap closure with a concave center commonly referred to as the "female" side

outie the side of the magnetic snap with a convex center commonly referred to as the "male" side

notch a small cut into the seam allowance, which allows fabric to bend at curves and corners

notions sewing supplies and equipment needed to complete a sewing project

quilt batting a soft, thick substance, usually made of wool, cotton, or another material that is stitched between two layers of fabric

seam allowance the remaining measurement of fabric left after sewing a seam

straight stitch stitching made with single forward stitches; the regular stitch that most sewing machines make; may or may not require a special presser foot

Resources

The materials used in this book are available at fine local crafts and fabric stores everywhere. Here is a listing of retailers and wholesalers to assist you in finding the closest supplier, or to assist in finding an item that is a little more difficult to get.

Fabric

M. Avery Designs
www.maverydesigns.com - Large supply of vintage and hard to find fabrics and notions.

eQuilter
www.equilter.com - Your Fabric Store for Quilting, Sewing, and Fashion

Reprodepot Fabrics
www.reprodepotfabrics.com - selection of wonderful vintage reproduction and retro fabrics

Buy Fabrics Online
www.buyfabricsonline.com - Buyfabricsonline.com is the only online ecommerce solution that is solely focused on the Alexander Henry Fabrics print collection.

Oilcloth International
www.oilcloth.com - source for quality oilcloth products.

Hancock Fabrics
www.hancockfabrics.com - Hancock Fabrics offers a large selection of fabric, quilting fabric, upholstery fabric and more. This site also has a store locator to find the nearest retail location.

Joann Fabric and Craft Stores
www.joann.com - Fabric and craft store.

Exotic Silks
www.exoticsilks.com - Wholesale silk at low prices

Michaels Arts, Crafts, & More
www. michaels.com

Hardware

M. Avery Designs
www.maverydesigns.com - Buy purse making supplies including purse handles, fabric, snaps, bag feet, Make your Own Handbag Kits and more.

National Webbing
www.nationalwebbing.com - Good source for webbing, nylon webbing, cotton webbing, straps, zippers, and more.

S. Axelrod Co.
www.axelrodco.com - Findings for Jewelry; Trims / Ornaments / Hardware / Chain for Manufacturers of Apparel, Home Decor, Leather Goods and Crafts; and Embellishments for Scrapbooking and Crafts.

A. C. Moore
www.acmoore.com - A good source for sewing notions including interfacing, batting, embellishments, lace, trim, etc.

UMX Fashion Supplies
www.umei.com - Specializing in purse supplies including purse handles, frames, purse chains, magnetic snaps, bag feet, hooks, and more.

Index